The Celestial Realm

The Celestial Realm

Molly Hennigan

eriu

First published in the UK by Eriu
An imprint of Black & White Publishing Group
A Bonnier Books UK company

4th Floor, Victoria House,
Bloomsbury Square,
London, WC1B 4DA

Owned by Bonnier Books
Sveavägen 56, Stockholm, Sweden

 – @eriu_books

– @eriubooks

Hardback – 978-1-80418-406-6
Ebook – 978-1-80418-445-5

A CIP catalogue of this book is available from the British Library.

Typeset by IDSUK (Data Connection) Ltd
Printed and bound by Clays Ltd, Elcograf S.p.A.

1 3 5 7 9 10 8 6 4 2

Eriu is an imprint of Bonnier Books UK
www.bonnierbooks.co.uk

*For my great grandmother Cissie,
and every other person lost in these
institutions, past and present*

Contents

The Celestial Realm

THE FIRST MONTH OR SO OF EACH STINT IN THE PSYCH WARD WAS PUNCTUATED BY DAILY MATERIAL AND IMMATERIAL REQUESTS, AS WELL AS THE USUAL MESSAGES FROM ON HIGH: 'Clarins Doux Peel. LoUis Armstrng Wat a wunderful World. You are a Duality! ... composed of two parts! ... what you "are" cannot be diminished! ... and nothing could make up for what you're "not"!' The material requests were for comfort – to make my grandmother Phil's bed in her basement ward feel like a home. The immaterial requests

1

were songs that God would've sung to her that day or the night before. Phil would want to know all the lyrics, the better to steep herself in His love through the voices of Petula Clark, John McCormack, Etta James, Rihanna or Luke Kelly. The remaining messages were streams of consciousness flowing from Him to her and on through the spiritual magic of unlimited data to my mother and me. Playing the songs for her on YouTube while she lay in her bed reacting was love in action. It was unorthodox love, but what Phil marvelled at, I did too, in my own way. She marvelled at God. He loved her. She told me they were like eighteen-year-old lovers. She giggled at the ceiling of her ward when He said intimate things. She couldn't get over how intelligent He was. He would say really smart things, she said. She would repeat them. They were smart.

Julia Kristeva says that it is possible to over-come or 'curb' mourning in a way that gives one 'a subliminatory hold over the lost Thing'. She explores this possibility through the idea of prosody, through the idea of rhythmic oscilla-tion. 'The language beyond language that inserts into the sign the rhythm and alliterations of semiotic processes.'

In her intonation and lilt, when singing and also speaking, Phil stresses and rhythmically implies power and loss, mourning and epiphany, all at once. The heights and depths of ethereal meaning for her drag and surge through her vocal cords, sharing with me through sound a taste of the pain and beauty she feels. She has been consistently manic and high for some time now, but the framework of a single song seems to act as a microcosm of what bipolar disorder has been for her over the years. In just a couple of minutes, pure elation drops to despair.

'*Enchanted by her beauty rare, I gazed in pure delight*'—her eyes are glinting; she is giddy—'*till round an angle of the road, she vanished from my sight*'—she waves her hot, swollen hand—'*but ever since I sighing say, as I that scene recall, the grace of God about you and your auld plaid shawl. I'll seek her all through Galway and I'll seek her all through Clare* ... this is the bit He's after singing to me now ... *I will seek her all through Galway and seek her* ...' She pauses.

Her lip drops and her face seems heavy with a confused sadness. She wrinkles her nose up and whispers through tears to God, 'Wait, I'm not ready ... *seek her all through Clare*'—she sings nervously now. She seems uncomfortable; her voice disappears with crying as she mouths the words—'*I'll search for tale or tiding of my traveller everywhere*'—she's crying heavily now—'*For peace of mind I'll never find*'—rubbing her tummy and crying—'*until my own I call*'—pauses, mouth bunched, then moves quickly through the next bit in tears—'*that little Irish cailín in her auld plaid shawl*'—sniffles, takes a deep breath and continues crying quietly. 'Stop,' she whispers to herself or to Him, I'm not sure. 'Stop!'—holding both hands together tight, rubbing each other—'So, He's got me now.'

There's a dizziness to the whole thing. It is otherworldly. She comes back to the room. 'So He's got me now,' she says, looking at me with the saddest eyes. She has the weight of different worlds on her shoulders. It is real for her and she is trying to exist in two spaces. To migrate from one universe to another measuring their relative loneliness and judging where best to set up camp. It looks agonising.

Alongside the physical pain of Phil's recurring kidney infections – then her frequent falls; then her breast cancer and mastectomy – is a lucidity that is new. I often wonder if the physical pain of her mid-eighties is a disc pressing on the nerve of her lucidity, releasing the part of her brain that will engage with the truth of her reality. I feel guilty even saying that. *Truth of her reality*. I have been complicit in layering fiction over truth for her. To be a patient in a psychiatric ward is like dying. You are stripped of autonomy while any sense of self is bleached and sterilised – you begin to question what your 'autonomy' even is, or what you would want if you had it. Would you want to leave? Why would you leave everything you know? Patterns you have been forcibly bent to fit into. There is nothing out there that you know. You have either forgotten all of the amazing foods you used to cook, or you don't see yourself as the same person who used to cook them. Days drag into a blind repetition of habits and compliances. You will be rewarded at meal times for engaging. Rewards will vary from a smile to a verbal congratulations but even in the dopiest throes of lithium-induced stupor you will know in your slurred response that these rewards are not sincere. These people are not sincere. Individually, some are. But they are feeding into a system that is designed to control and subjugate you. You are an inmate. You know this. Your family who visit know this but they distract themselves and you from that truth by bringing you fresh fruit and dressing gowns and chocolates and you feed again into their self-absorbed need to feel helpful, to feel righteous. You thank them for the things they bring and the time they give. They don't go home feeling better. There is no lack of sincerity there, but now as you lie in a ward in Tallaght Hospital having 'possibly' – they say – fallen out of your bed in the lockdown psychiatric unit in which you live, there is nothing sincere about family having visited you there and brought things you like to eat and to wear.

Phil is eighty-five. She has been dying for forty years. She has been revived at times, spending stints in her own home, and has even been well enough to take me out for drives in her red Mini. When I was a young child, we often went swimming together at the local leisure centre. I would stand beside her, no taller than her bare hip bone, and watch her put on two tight swimming hats to protect her hair from the chlorine. She looked like a model. Sometimes she also swam with a snorkel and paid no attention to me, mortified and bobbing in the far corner of the pool. Afterwards she would feed me cheese sandwiches on homemade brown bread that was so stodgy it stuck to the roof of my mouth. I once caught a glimpse of myself in the glass cabinet that had the expensive swimming togs and hats in it as I tried to tease the bread down with my tongue and the vein-laced rib on the bottom of my tongue matched my bloodshot eyes.

For the most part, though, she was dying. Slowly. In truth, she was never really in her house in the last few years, and any time she was there, food just stacked up in the kitchen and rotted while she posted sticky notes all around the house for God. And for Satan sometimes, who for a spell took the form of her neighbours' two-year-old boy. Despite this, she was happy.

*

Phil doesn't like physical affection. She doesn't love you because you don't exist. You are a projection of something. She doesn't care if you're sick because she doesn't believe in cancer. She doesn't care if you have something important coming up – a busy week, a daunting appointment, a divorce – because she believes the world is going to end in the morning. Every morning. Unwavering belief. She won't associate with you as family. She doesn't really believe she is anything to anyone bar having acted the part for a higher purpose, which she is now fulfilling. You can now be disposed of. She doesn't tell you she loves you. Nobody knows love like her and God. It is just them. She can't be sure that you will be saved. All she knows is that 'her and God are the Celestial Realm'. I might burn tomorrow morning in the fires of hell, she tells me and my mother, as I bring her two oranges from the bag of oranges I have in the car because she won't let me bring her in a full bag of oranges because she won't need that many because the world is ending in the morning.

'Okay,' I say, as I peel an orange.

Something instinctively maternal and also naïve in my mother takes offence to this.

'Well, why, Phil? Why won't she be saved?' My mother is in no way religious, but she seems to have been sucked into the narrative.

I frown over at her. 'It's grand.'

'No, it's not. Why is my daughter going to burn in the fires of hell, Phil?'

'I'm not saying she will, Deirdre, I'm just saying she might. It's nothing to do with me.'

'It is. She's your granddaughter.'

'Haha, no she's not.'

I find myself almost laughing with Phil. 'Mam, it's grand. Thank you though.'

'C'mon, Molly. I need to go. I have to get out of here. We're going, come on.'

That would happen regularly. Phil would unintentionally wind my mam up and she would be wound tight.

*

A few months ago, she began touching her forehead against ours as we were leaving at the end of visits. I couldn't remember the last time she touched me before that. My mam and I both welled up a little the first time, waiting in the corridor that one nurse locked us into before a nurse at the other end of the corridor could let us out. This emotional vacuum. If we brought that emotion out into the car and onto the M50 and into my mam's new apartment it would ruin everything. It would ruin that evening. It would make it impossible for me to go home the next morning and leave her there, alone. I had a sickly shiver and a damp, now cooling feeling under my armpits. It was stress sweat. Particularly sour. Period sweat is pretty disgusting and pungent and sex sweat is quite nice and musky but stress sweat is just bitter. That's the one that will ruin your clothes. I had no appetite and felt a bit dizzy but suggested we get fish and chips on the way home.

'Oh yeah, lovely. What time is it? I think there's two *Emmerdale*s on tonight.'

'Aw deadly.' I wasn't being sarcastic but there was a pause.

We both know I don't watch soaps any more and I think that carries some layered meaning for my mother. It creates some heavy distance between us, which might sound trivial but feels sad. It was all I wanted to do that evening though.

'That'll be nice,' I follow up.

It's still a bit lacklustre. I ask about a character I remember; a child when I last saw the show. She is now pregnant and runs a business. I don't know if I'm more sad that it has been that long since I've spent some quality time with my mother, or that the measure of it is a fictional soap character growing up.

*

I was born on St Brigid's Day and people always ask why I wasn't called Brigid. I always liked that my birthday was the first of February for this reason and also because it was the start of spring. I still like it for these reasons. But as a child, or even teenager, these things didn't mean much. They were just conversation pieces. St Brigid wasn't really celebrated enough for me

11

to find much meaning in sharing my birthday with her day, and a new season went unnoticed when I was shipped back and forth in the same school buses and cars to the same places year-round. For a few months, I knew that it was dark when I went to school and dark again when I came out, but I didn't care. The warm entrapment of childhood numbed me to the elements since the house I came home to already had the lights on. And, if it didn't, a taller person was with me and was able to reach for the switch. It never really felt like I came into a dark room as a child.

The psychiatric unit is like that too. All hospitals are, I suppose. Always on. Lights always switched on, heating always going. People always there. Never officially closed. Phil is cooped up in this seasonless, sterile, fluorescent house. The setting sun pokes through the closed blinds in her kitchen, beaming a line across dancing dust particles. But she isn't there to see it. I visit her in the winter and she says I should probably get on the road soon, it must be so late. It is only around five, late afternoon, getting dark. She has no concept of time, really, or rather, she has an institutionalised concept but not a natural one – it is punctuated and marked by meals she is brought. She has lost her feeling for time and light and seasons. So we don't talk about winter or summer or longer or shorter evenings. And so we don't talk about spring being a turning point for that, and it being my birthday, and it being St Brigid's Day. And so, somehow, we have never spoken either about the fact that her mother, my great-grandmother, known as Sissy, was actually called Brigid.

Sissy died in Grangegorman Mental Hospital. In his work *Irish Insanity: 1800–2000*, Damien Brennan discusses the secondary functions of asylums in Ireland: 'These institutions were often the largest provider of local employment within communities,' he says. 'This employment included roles directly related to the care of the insane, such as keeper and nurse but also included roles related to the physical and administrative structure of the asylum such as builders, plumbers, store keepers, book keepers and gardeners.' Maintaining this employment required patients to keep the asylums open; generally, people were committed if they didn't conform or contribute – economically or practically – to society. A society that was still reeling from the effects of the Famine, trying to pack away any loose ends and hide what looked unseemly. A doddery uncle, a pregnant single woman, postnatal depression, anything. Modelling ourselves on the oppressor – put the outcasts in there, and give the rest of us a job cleaning or building it.

My grandmother was twelve when her mam, Sissy, died. My grandaunt, Vera, was only two. Sissy lived in one of the most notorious asylums in the history of this small country. We had the global lead on psychiatric incarcerations per capita, beating the former Soviet Union even as we were being drained of population after the Famine. 'The population of Ireland almost halved between 1841 and 1911, decreasing from 8,175,124 to 4,390,319,' writes Brennan. 'This is the same period that saw the institutional residency of the "insane" increase more than seven times, from 3,498 to 24,655.'

The figures are so staggering they say the only reasonable answer would be an epidemic of mental illness. Rather, the epidemic was of mental conformity to the strict and narrow rules defining what was accepted, what was normal. The line was so narrow and unforgiving it wound back upon itself: it became the sickness. People were incarcerated for all types of reasons – sane people were committed if they were the black sheep of the family; if they had moral standards outside of the social norm, financial disagreements, personal views on arranged marriage. All reasonable, sound and independent thoughts. Sissy had children, was married, fit the aesthetic. However, the full range of emotions from anger to love to jealousy were also ripe for manipulation in the process of incarceration, so essentially any person experiencing any feeling in any perceived sense of the extreme was fair game. Brennan again: 'Insanity was a vague, changing and all-encapsulating concept which could be applied to most social difficulties so as to facilitate and rationalise the admission of a family member to an asylum.'

I don't have much detail about Sissy. She died in a hospital whose records are difficult to obtain. Archival work is being done to preserve the rooms full of patients' personal belongings – their handbags make it seem as if they were plucked from the street and committed. This is important work, but just speaks to the sheer volume of incarceration and the ease of follow-through upon accusation. Sissy belongings might be among them. There could be something in her bag to soothe a teething baby she thought she was going home to, lipstick, a key to a house she thought she would sleep in that night, or at the very least lie awake in with restless children.

Sissy is a figment of my imagination. I know she existed and she is part of the reason I am here imagining her, but still, that's all I can do. There's nothing left of her; only the history of her context and us, now. Becoming acquainted with her through a reading of the psychiatric history of Ireland is jarring. Her history and our present moment, clashing in theory but meshing in reality. Her baby is being hurt in the same rooms now. Female lineage in Ireland feels like a wet, mucky, bloody rag to cling to. It is steadfast, durable. It is tangible, the evidence exists, the stains of suffering are there, but there is no information. Whose blood is where?

I have Sissy's long-form death certificate. I can run my fingers along the ink of the writing that says she died at Grangegorman Mental Hospital. I can think of the fact that it was written in the building where she died. I can tell from the dated signature that it was written the day after she died. That she died on 6 October. The signature, qualification and residence of the informant: Katheryn O'Donnell, inmate, Grangegorman Mental Hospital. Inmate. Incarcerated.

The language of mental healthcare in the late 1800s through to the 1940s was designed to 'quieten the patient'. Procedures as unthinkable as lobotomies and insulin-induced comas were forms of treatment; the desired outcome was silence. The year Sissy died in Grangegorman was when, according to the *Irish Medical Times*, lobotomy was introduced there. We talk about silencing Irish women and it is almost always metaphoric, or rather representative, of a particular type of non-hearing. We talk about the female Irish writers whose voices we haven't heard, whose books we haven't read, studied or situated appropriately within the canon. We talk about women who were politically active but not remembered justly. Let's also talk about the women's voices that were physically silenced. The women whose ability to communicate was severed by drilling into the skull. Men too, of course. Minorities and vulnerable people who were deemed 'idiots, lunatics and retards'.

The intersection between these barbaric forms of 'treatment' and the Irish habit of incarcerating sane and healthy people into asylums is a monumental historic travesty. Much like the very nature of the procedure, a 'desired outcome of silence' has persisted around this particular nadir in Irish history. Brennan details the various causes and recorded numbers for incarceration as noted in the 1837 'Inspectors of Lunatic Asylums Report', with 1,639 people incarcerated for moral causes, 2,006 for physical causes, 1,898 for hereditary causes and 4,577 for unknown causes.

There are blocks and pacifiers all around to quieten the voices that try to shed light on historical injustices. Often, we don't even know what the problems are, and so we cannot begin to address them. This is no accident. But we are the offspring of these injustices, and dissociation is one of the most common things Irish people do. 'They' ran the Magdalene laundries, 'they' performed lobotomies, 'they' killed or left people brain-dead after insulin-induced comas. In Ireland we can say 'they' and 'we' because 'they' are almost always the Church or the colonial oppressor. This social habit of repeated, and sometimes justified, blaming has become a tool in keeping this part of our history submerged. But it is not always someone else's fault. 'They' aren't only the Church or the oppressor when it comes to the asylum system in Ireland; institutionalisation persisted after respective colonial and religious holds began to loosen. 'Rather than reforming and closing these institutions as symbols of an oppressive colonial legacy,' Brennan writes, 'asylums were expanded within the Irish Republic to the extent that Ireland had the highest rate of mental hospital usage internationally.'

We talk about the relationship between State and Church in Ireland. We talk about war and oppression and famine: events that changed the fabric of our country; that trampled the system we had, forcing us to start again. Everything has been broken and has begun again, except our asylum system. It lurks. Cold, towering buildings sleeping over towns and villages where we do driving tests and get X-rays and collect children from school and donate to Dogs Trust. These institutions blend into the skyline of Ireland, and have withstood every national catastrophe we have faced.

*

Phil's condition has deteriorated markedly in recent months. When I visit, I feel guilty about where I am coming from or leaving for. My guilt is tied into how broad my frames of context are and how narrow are hers. She cannot move much in bed or stand up by herself. She cannot answer the door to see it is me, so my visiting borders on intrusion. She might not want to see me just then. Dignity is compromised; wounded in the cross-fire between my wide, roaming existence and her walled one, in the crossfire between unsolicited visits and a policing of personal decisions.

A nurse who doesn't work on Phil's ward but who is passing through the corridor offers to buzz me in as I wait at the door. Displaying due diligence, she comes with me to alert a duty nurse that I am on the ward. I see why that is necessary, but she is nonetheless a little rushed and loud. She is speaking at a high volume in the hopes that a nurse will appear from the TV room or nurses' station or someone's ward. She is bordering on shouting, 'Phyllis's granddaughter has come to visit. Phyllis's granddaughter is here.' Having my visit announced like it is a rarity makes me feel painfully distant from my grandmother. A nurse from the ward does arrive; she nods, and everyone disbands. I am left to my own devices.

The door into Phil's room is held open by a chair. I walk in to find her fast asleep, lying on her right side with both hands tucked under her right cheek and just her bare toes covered by the blanket, which is pushed back to the bottom of the bed. She is in a deep sleep and the position of her hands and pillow are squishing her lips to create a resting pucker face. The soft lines that her lips fold into with the pressure of flesh and pillow trick me into thinking she is content. It looks like a peaceful sleep and I let myself believe that. It also stops me from waking her. It would feel unkind. Also, she would only really be coming around when I have to leave, which is cruel. I sit on the chair beside her bed, indecisive. A nurse walks by and I ask him if she slept last night. He says she did, which tempts me to wake her after all. I text my partner, Rónán, to consult. 'Definitely wake her. She'll be annoyed if she misses you!' Sitting on the edge of her bed, I try gently to rouse her. She wakes enough to see it is me and then closes her eyes again. They have given her something to ease her anxiety so she is drowsy. She has had a rough week. She is in and out of sleep and I'm happy she knows I'm there. I rub between her shoulder blades and the warm glow of sun on the back of her navy cardigan is comforting. I rub in concentric circles for maybe six or seven minutes and I feel friction and dizziness in each cell of my hand. I pause to let the tingle subside. Her hair has fallen to the side of her face. The strands lie hardened and dry on her cheek in front of her ear. I slowly warm them in my hand and ease them back behind her ear, tucking them into the crevice at her lobe; the crevice that feels soft and comforted by a gentle touch but if poked accidentally releases some kind of sour sensation in the glands of your neck. I am careful.

I stroke through the hair elsewhere on her head that is a little greasier and smoother. The smell of hair and scalp is the most naturally comforting. It is the smell I associate with the aftermath of heavy crying. It is the first thing your senses notice when they finally come round. When the sun shines warm on the pillow and heats the natural oils in your scalp they smell comforting, the way the soil turned over in flower beds smells comforting. I breathe deep and keep stroking her hair. Her skin looks grey and she is sad. Sadder than I have ever seen her.

'I am having a lot of trouble at the moment, Molly,' she says while I look down at the side of her cheek, rubbing her back again.

'I know.' I don't prompt in any direction but I expect her to continue.

She closes her eyes again.

I know she has been asking my mam to save her during recent visits and crying as my mam leaves. I am prepared for that, or so I believe. More truthfully, I am anticipating it but I know I could never be prepared.

'Sorry, I'm so tired. I just keep sleeping. Just need to sleep again.'

'Do sleep,' I say. 'I'll sit here a while longer and then I won't wake you when I leave.'

'They gave me something to calm me down. It feels nice.'

'Good, that's good. Just go with that relaxing feeling while it's here.'

She falls back into a deep sleep, her soft body heaving with deep breathing. A few minutes pass.

She wakes again and needs the toilet. I take her into the bathroom and she wants me to stay. It is a new context for us both. Our identities and their relation to one another are already formed and solid, but they stretch into new territory in this space. I lift her from her wheelchair and sit her onto the toilet bowl. She seems calm and dignified and I feel close to her.

I use her soap, which reminds me of her house and of me as a child. It is masking another smell in her bathroom that suggests diarrhoea and my immediate reaction is concern. I don't know much but I've always had a sense that these small fluctuations in bodily functions can mean more in old age; can be more grave. In recent months smells of bodily fluids have become increasingly associated with care for me and I wonder somewhere in the back of my mind what that means. There is something about this newfound prioritising of the safety and cleanliness of the bodies around me that makes me think I am ready to have a baby. Also the fact that the name Mabel has been sitting at the front of my mind for a full week and even gave me a surge of excitement the other evening at the prospect of calling a little blank face that and telling other people that that was her face's name. It all feels like a slow, inevitable acceptance on which I don't want to put language yet. In conversation at least. The timeframe of it all seems pressured but slow-moving. Like wisdom teeth coming through.

I don't think Phil cares that she won't meet a baby I might have in the future and I don't think of that potential as a life right now anyway. I do find it difficult that I might love someone else as much as her someday. Someone who she won't have met. Someday when she is no longer here for me to love. In loving Phil and learning about her mother I feel like the next round of life and death in my family will be the change I resist most. I once asked Phil what it was like to give birth. She answered dismissively: 'It was all water and legs.'

Liverpool Lullaby

PHIL NEVER ANSWERED TO THE NAME OF GRAND-MOTHER, OR ANY VARIATION OF IT. Our kinship was always a step removed for this lack of an affectionate name but the distance never felt cold or empty. Instead, it provided clarity as we travelled abreast through different ages. The same people always. The skin of her face was maternal in a withdrawn way too. Once you touched it, tacky from make-up, it warmed straight away. It was cool only to the initial touch, like the back of your arms above your elbow, how they would get cold on summer evenings and you mightn't notice for a while. Until they were touched by a warm hand or your jumper sleeve or the bus seat. That was the nicest warmth for coming so soon after an unnoticed cool breeze. Phil's is the nicest love for being adjacent to such independence.

There is a distance of its own making between my mother and Phil, though I cannot account for its shape and size. I can't assume it has birthed a clarity of identity and dependence between them like I have come to know. I wasn't there for the years when they tried to be a conventional mother and daughter and I haven't asked for documentary detail, though I have heard snippets of it in natural conversation. They are the natural types of conversations that only come up because you live with your mother and because she is your mother, and even then, when you are having them, it doesn't seem real that you are or ever will again. Conversations without developments – just succinct, base facts – as she does your roots or drives somewhere with you. 'Well I lived with the McLysaghts for a while when she was sick,' she says. 'But they were lovely. They would let me help in the garden. That's why I love gardening.' It feels strange to hear things like that out of the blue. I think with sadness of the photos of me at six or seven standing in front of her tall rows of sweet pea in the back garden. I think of my view that day too. My mother standing behind the camera. Her familiar face proud for a now unfamiliar reason. I think of the days I've seen her spend in the garden, catering to her flowers and plants and I try to reconcile that happy memory with its origin, which I've just learned is rooted in pain.

The concept of caring for a child versus the capacity to do so was something I mixed up in my value system as a teenager. I think I only valued the former for a while. Basing it on what one is able for throws the parameters of success wide open. When I handwrote the notes for the affidavit for my mother's divorce in 2015 I discovered that my father, instead of going to get milk for me as a newborn, went instead to an early house to drink, leaving my mother alone with a new child in an isolated setting. I had to distance myself from that newborn. The news was not of me. I was transcribing the events, had a job to do. I was trying to shape words on the page in a way that meant she would be able to keep the couch we sat on while she told me these stories. 'Respondent was due home with urgent supplies for baby but went to an early house leaving both Applicant and newborn baby in need.' I was trying to ape the performative utterance that had got us stuck here in the first place: *I do*. To utter the sentence is to do it. I wanted, at the end of it all, for there to be a vow of divorce. A performative utterance of departing, an unsticking. There wasn't. And so I documented the day, and the days each side of the event instead.

Two nights before the court date the bottom shelf in a kitchen cupboard broke. Tupperware containers slid down, putting pressure on the cereal boxes on the bottom row. They spilled onto the floor. Two mornings later, as we headed to court, we stepped on loose cornflakes and porridge oats. No one had cleaned them up. My mother always kept the cereal on the bottom shelf to encourage independence. So that I could get up early as a young child and feed myself, mind myself.

At the court there was no parting vow and I was empty of words just then. I photographed everything in the days before the hearing. My photograph of the spilled porridge and loose Tupperware shows the broken oven handle I had forgotten. The particular speckle of the floor tiles and countertops I now, upon reflection, realise I despised. I could feel something close heavy in my mind when I looked at the dark word of the press. Could feel how temporary and collapsible the whole family endeavour was when I zoomed in to find a small screw camouflaged on the kitchen tile, the small screw tasked with preventing the shelf from folding in on itself, knocking cereal onto the floor, crunching under my foot, and recalling a bone-deep memory of independence only ever being commended. Only ever independence being commended. Another photo from the morning of the court date shows a navy and green razor in the bathroom sink and a long thick clump of my mam's cobalt-blue hair that streels slick and thin up the side of the sink bowl and slithers out. Her hair was falling out from stress. The next photo is of her sitting in front on me in a coffee shop in Naas, directly across the road from the courthouse. Her hair is tied tightly in a black headband and she has grown her roots out so that only a peak of mousy-brown hair comes through at the forehead. There was talk, through her solicitor, that bright-blue hair would damage her credibility. They didn't mind telling her this. Even though the barrister had the records in her hands of their years-long abusive relationship, she didn't mind telling my mother, as she repeatedly pulled at her headband, that my father was handsome. That the judge liked handsome men. That the judge would like how handsome he was.

*

When I was a child my mother used to sing the 'Liverpool Lullaby' by Stan Kelly to me, but she always swapped out the word 'scruffy' for 'pretty':

> You look so pretty lying there,
> Strawberry jam tart in your hair,
> In all the world you haven't a care,
> And I have got so many ...

I knew my mam had so many cares when she sang me this lullaby. My room, painted yellow with light-grey curtains, was the scene of perpetual daytime where, as the youngest child on the estate, I lay in bed listening to the older kids playing into the bright night. The yellow wallpaper was lit up by the late sun setting. There were flecks on the curtains that reminded me of sore throats, the room a big heated Lemsip. She would sing this song to me and I knew what some of her concerns were. I knew my father was not good to her. I knew he was an alcoholic. And I knew he could read better than her. In fact, I knew I could read better than her so I knew she was stuck. That was enough to know at that age. More than enough, probably. More than other, older kids probably knew about their parents, I thought, as they continued playing rounders out on the green. My cheeks burned with jealousy listening to the echo of their voices. I could tell who was batting and running by the direction of the voices. I was jealous and angry but their voices ringing in my ears were drowned out by hers singing, calling me a mucky kid and running her fingers through my hair, which hadn't been touched by her hand all day and which now brought me back, drowsy, from where I thought I wanted to be.

My instinct at the time leaned toward protection. Initially, there was a belief in it and, later, an embodiment of it. The first time you hear a word you don't know, you'll slip it into a context you can find. It is almost always innocent or positive. Though it is out of place, it is something you understand. The line in the 'Liverpool Lullaby' – *'When he finds out the things that you did, you'll get a belt from your da'* – to me meant a seatbelt. Protection. My childhood became a series of misunderstandings and recontextualisations. Save me became save yourself became I'll save you became wait I can't. It was like a loop that shortened. Save me dropped off first.

Save me, save yourself, I'll save you, I can't.

Save yourself, I'll save you, I can't.

I'll save you, I can't.

I can't.

I knew I knew things because she shared them with me but I still felt like I was keeping a secret from her by understanding them. I don't think she thought about how much I paid attention to the things she said either. My reception of it all didn't go any particular direction other than developing into a certain knowledge of my mother and a reshaping of my love for her into a desire to protect, but without the resources to do so. I cried some evenings when she sang the 'Liverpool Lullaby' to me. She sometimes asked why – I never answered. Other times she presumed to know, telling me I'd see my friends tomorrow. On rare occasions she would do neither, just drop her hand from my scalp to my cheek, wipe away a tear and continue singing. You sing to yourself too when you sing aloud, and her walls came down sometimes. It was all held in that room, like us. The orange sun setting on yellow walls, the soft singing voice and soft hands running through wisps of white, young hair was a refuge for us both.

I don't know if she has memories like that, or as warm. And if she does, I don't know if they were provided by her own mother. There are thirty years between me and my mother. The same between her and Phil. I've had my run as a daughter. She hasn't, I don't think. But I think she might be getting it now. It may well be too late to have any shaping effect but, for all the painful reality it brings, the lucidity that Phil has recently slipped into does allow her to recognise my mother's care and hard work. And there is some joy in that. If my mother did her giving when I was young, and is more of a friend now, she has never stopped being a daughter. She is teaching me how, and in doing so has never really stopped mothering either. Not even at times in our past when we both thought she had. Being in every action Phil's daughter makes her more my mother in turn.

*

My mother is a hairdresser and I have only ever had my hair done in the kitchen of our family home. When she bleaches and cuts my hair now, I try not to let myself fall into appreciating the feeling of her fingers on my scalp again. I find my skull too preoccupied with the pain in my jaw from unclenching my teeth that were grinding all night. I find my mind too distracted by the shortness of her nightdress, seen when she absent-mindedly takes off her dressing gown and shows parts of her legs I haven't known for years. I find myself sad that no one else knows these parts. Sad that they are so unfamiliar to me yet I am the person who knows them best. My scalp stings so much from the bleach that drinking tea while waiting for the bleach to lift feels like the hot liquid is being sipped through enamel-stripped teeth. Like it is my teeth being bleached. There is always that sense too, after the haircut, and its bluntness, of a finality or distance. People go to the hairdresser and pay them and leave feeling ready to face the world, or their world. There is, more often than not, a sense when my hair is done that I am leaving my world. That my mother is dressing or preparing me to go somewhere she isn't coming. That she might put her dressing gown back on again later if she gets cold, or the damp creeps in, and I wouldn't know.

For months leading up to the divorce she would wear her dressing gown in the daytime over her clothes. Sometimes she would have work later or be meeting a friend for coffee so it was always temporary. I read it as something pacifying or self-soothing, shrouding her. Some

St Brigid's cloak that was actually a bright-red Penneys dressing gown. It smelled in unequal parts damp, from having been taken off the radiator too early, and sweet, from having been sprayed with perfume to try and mask the dampness. It mostly failed. When I would meet her in town, or if she came to see a performance in the concert hall where I worked, the brown- and wine-toned make-up I had been so taken with as a child meant little. I would be arrested more so now, upon hugging her, by the sense that she smelled not of sweet perfume but of a damp, cheap dressing gown, to which she would return in a matter of hours. Truthfully, she wore it during the day because there was a stalemate between her and my father about turning the heating on. Neither wanted to pay for the other's warmth. Both chose to condition the other's discomfort, an approach that kept them strangely tethered to one another.

*

Narrative gaps in lived experience are down to trauma, my therapist tells me. I stare back at her on my laptop screen with the curtain drawn behind me, hiding remotes, papers, clips, a stereo and mugs on a wide windowsill. It is daytime and the brightness bursts through the closed blind, silhouetting my head and obscuring my features. I am in my mother's apartment in Clane. I am here alone. My mother has moved to Liverpool and I stay here sometimes for short stints. It is damp to the core and I seem to spend my days emptying the water from the large plug-in dehumidifier that I drag from room to room. The washing machine is broken and I hand-wash all my clothes and towels. Deep pools of water slush around different wash baskets that I use for cold rinses after the main wash in the bath. My right wrist weakens quickly from wringing towels dry. I broke it when I was eleven and a boy in my class told me – we were playing kiss-chasing – that the yard wall was den. I ran full speed into the yard wall. I used my multicoloured scarf as a sling on the way to the hospital. It was a warm day and I remember sitting on the curb outside Tallaght Hospital with my mother, admiring my new cast and waiting for her to finish speaking to my dad on the phone. Whenever we were out of the house together, either for a long time or to an unusual place, I always felt at the end of the day that perhaps we could keep going instead of driving back to the house. Rather than feeling inhibited by the cast, I felt it bestowed a certain agency and maturity on me; a mark, somehow, of endurance. I only ever wanted to be uninhibited and mature for my mother. I never thought that running face first into a wall, away from a sweaty bully who was scaring me, was an exhibition of agency. Never would've seen that act as demonstrating any capacity for independence. Never would've thought of myself as being on the receiving end of any smart decisions, or that I'd ever make any of them for myself.

My mother gets the boat over every few months and replaces all the hanging plastic dehumidifiers in the wardrobes. Everything is buoyed by water in a way that threatens mildew. I like to visit when she has already been here for a few days and dried the place out. She likes to do the same. We mop up sopping damp rooms for each other. We welcome each other into dry spaces, heating each other up. It is comforting at first, warming. Then it dries you out too. The liquid in your eyes disappears and your eyelids wrinkle and itch. We suck all the water out of the rooms and all life out of each other. We never see the difference between dehumidifying the apartment and suffocating in dry, hot air until our lips chap like the little white pieces of tissue paper that men stick on cut, shaved faces.

On the phone the other day, my mother told me that the clothes were *possing* coming out of the washing machine. Something lit up in me, attentive and nostalgic, at hearing that word again – *possing* – a burst and flare that dissipated into an unease. Anything I write about our relationship will be washed away. Anything that bleeds, trickles, gushes. Phil said that giving birth was all water and legs and I wrote it down. It will all become flush, the act and the sentence. Anything that is damp now will be submerged. Any corners where mildew settles will no longer converge. Everything will open up and go.

*

The camera roll on my phone is peppered with photos of my mam doing Phil's hair in hospital. I expect they will trace a visual path of Phil's health, but more than that they are monotonous, repetitive. Looking at them, I feel there is an intimacy there I can tap into. Intimacy I don't know how to approach or express with language, but that I can feel drawing me in. Maybe it arises from the fact of the repetition itself. The fact that I get to keep taking the same photo of them in different jumpers on different days, at different angles, in different light doing the same thing. The fact that the hair keeps growing. There was good hair when she was still walking. There was better hair when she was still walking and laughing. There was the best hair when she was still at home and curling tufts of it into a shape that was quintessentially feminine and elegant. There is bad hair now. Weak and brittle hair now, dry and wispy. My mother trims her fringe so that she can see the hospital clearly.

She does more than cut Phil's hair. She clips and then paints my grandmother's toenails red. I hold the bottle of nail polish for my mother to periodically dip into while Phil lies back in her hospital bed, speaking to us.

'I used to think you had to die to be with the angels, remember that, Deirdre, years ago? And I was sitting around saying, "I have to die now."'

'Mm, I remember that,' my mother mutters under her breath, seemingly distant. I can't tell if it's because she is concentrating on painting Phil's nails or because she doesn't want to recall that memory. Phil laughs as she reminisces. My mam looks tired.

'So I said, "I know what I'll do. That girl, what's-her-name round at the back road, she threw herself into the sea down in, em, Dún Laoghaire. I'll go down there and I'll throw *myself* into the sea." And he goes, "You WON'T."'

Her laugh rises an octave or two. I almost laugh.

'Did she do that?' my mam asks against the grate of nail file on chalked toenail.

Phil is still giggling as she answers, 'Yes.'

It is my mam who is in the real firing line here. Phil and I, in different ways, are removed from the story, its sombre nature. Phil laughs off the memory, residing now for the most part in another realm. I try to piece it together, knowing none of the moving parts. My mother shows the most concern. This neighbour is someone she would've known as a child. This account of drowning is only coming to her now.

'Now, there was a big question over whether it was an accident or whether she did it on purpose, but knowing her husband I'd say she did it on purpose.'

'Why, was he a bollocks?' my mam asks.

'Yeah, little bollocks.'

'In what way?'

'Just was. You'd know by him. Although I shouldn't be saying that. She was nice, wasn't she?'

'She was.'

My mam got a little bit of nail polish on the hard skin of Phil's toe. Nothing about her prompts it but I can't help but see her as a little girl in this scene. Can't help but see all the plummets and shafts of her childhood where there should have been steady ground. Her legs swing off the end of the high hospital bed. The closed bottle of polish I've been clutching since she finished is now warming in my hands. Phil's eyes are closed, almost opening now and then as raised eyebrows lift the lid a little. She is smirking. God is so charming. My mam's legs keep swinging. Her ankles look cold. It is cold in here today. My mam seems so settled sitting there at the end of the bed. I wonder how she spent the hours as a child. Like this, I imagine. I understand her patience now. Her acceptance of almost anything. Though endearing at times, it is mostly dangerous to be so accepting, I think. Even my advice, though I try to neutralise and flatten it, she takes blindly. That has always petrified me too.

I think of a letter she found recently, a letter my grandmother sent to her from St John of God psychiatric hospital. My mother was seven years old at the time. It was written on 9 April 1970.

Thursday
9/4/70

hello Deirdre,
are you
being a good girl for Daddy? Are you glad to be back at school? I'll be home soon to

walk to school with you. I hope you'll have a new poem for me when I get back. You are not to worry about me because I'm having a nice time here. I love you very much. I'll get you a lovely new pair of shoes when I come home.

XXXXX Mammy

My mother has told me stories of what it was like to be the child of that woman, at that time. Standing on the path outside Trinity College waiting for a bus together when my mother was eight, Phil pointed up to a small window at the top of a building on the street opposite and told her that was the room where she first had sex on her period. She explained what that meant. What that was like. Almost like a child herself, my mam had said.

My memories of being eight are safer. And the memories are true – I was safer. The woman who made my childhood safe is the eight-year-old whose mother told her some things she shouldn't and some things she should. Both out of affection, out of closeness. One skewed, misjudged. One painfully normal, maternal. *I'll get you a lovely new pair of shoes when I come home.* I cried with my mother when she found that letter. We cried a similar amount. I made myself stop when she did, then I went into the bathroom and cried some more. Once I'd finished I paused the dehumidifier, poured the heavy plastic box of water from it down the toilet, patted my face and went back into the hot, dry sitting room to my mother. The capacity to love is all that matters here. Everything else will wash away.

Healing Properties

I OFTEN THINK OF MY SISTER, KERRIE, AS MY
FIRST LOVE, BUT MY FIRST MEMORY OF THIS LOVE
COMES SO LATE. Comes after she left the house.
Six years between us meant we shared a primary
school but, both foregoing transition year, not a
secondary one. We were on a high-speed chase
through the education system. Trying to get out
as quickly as we could with as much intelligence
as possible so that we could escape that house.

One dark November afternoon I sat on the bus
home from school. It was a small bus, with the

same ten or fifteen students using it for years. We spanned different year groups and social hierarchies but lived on the same string of estates. A chain of estates that required a loop of the town that the bus driver was happy to travel each day because it traced, loosely, the places her teenage son would loiter. She mounted the curb one day in the middle of December when she realised it was her son and his friends who were pelting snowballs at us. She got out of the bus and chased him across a field, screaming her characteristically choice curses. We were left, half on the path, half on the road, parents in jeeps collecting schoolchildren beeping furiously at us. Her distant speck of a body running almost completely out of sight and none of us with any concept of a steering wheel or gear stick, sitting and waiting awkwardly in the long drone of overlapping beeps. So while we were different, we students had bonded in strange moments like these.

It was the following November, on the dark trip home around 4.20 p.m. with the windows fogged up, streetlights already on an hour or so, that a love for my sister caught me off guard. She wasn't there. Was in college now, gone. But one girl on the bus had a sore throat. She was a couple of years older than me. She told everyone that morning on the bus, Strepsils in hand and her perfect ponytail swishing against the clear, fog-less window as the cold sun rose and the morning dew receded. We listened to her but everything was fresh and seemed light. Now, at 4.20 p.m., she climbed out of the dark cold and into the small bus. Made her way to the back, as hierar-chy allowed. Her cheeks, I noticed, as she clam-bered down the small aisle between seats, were a familiar rosy colour. I looked at them while she spoke until, and because of that, they deepened to a scarlet red and were no longer a shade rec-ognisable to me. Her throat was killing her, she said. She reached over the hill of her huge school-bag, all honours textbooks inside, and grabbed her water bottle with old teeth marks scuffing and circling the lid. As she opened her mouth to drink, her tongue showed itself, a light layer of some fuzz on it. Some hint of infection or some-thing. Her eyes were tired and her cheeks, now that she had settled on the hot bus, continued to flame up brighter. A different face entirely but each of these colours and textures on it, inside this small safe bus caught me, like a gust of wind, off guard. I could feel myself starting to cry and turned to plant my forehead on the window. My high ponytail pushed against the headrest, painful and tweaking the thin plastic hairband that caught individual hairs at angles and yanked them. My hair was thick with grease. It was too difficult to wash. It was not very long any more but anything about my body and its maintenance was difficult. Being attentive to myself seemed to run the risk of being, or becoming, increasingly aware; of my surroundings, of the relentless years of screaming, of the fear that was carried in my body, of the mild, soft incompetence of my mother in the face of my abusive father. I fixed the bobbin and thought away from my hair. Thought back to my sister. Back to the details of the face behind me, throat sore, face red, sad and tired. And I bit my lip to keep back the tears.

I loved my sister so much. I only realised it now. On a new level at least. A level that was more than parentally prescribed affection of 'this is your sister. Love her.' This love was sad. It was 'my poor sister. I love her.' It wasn't poor me, poor us. I was looking, through the fogged-up window, at the peripheral glare of a red traffic light. After it turned green, I would have to get off the bus. I would have to walk into the house. I would probably have to wash my hair. I couldn't think of me. Couldn't do poor me. Couldn't love me. But I cried that night after my shower, in bed. Thinking of my sister.

Being born into my immediate family was less like being delivered into the middle of an on-going conversation, and more like being dropped into the middle of a screaming match. A years-long aggressive fight, the start of which could never be traced. From the off, a cacophony of sound. How to think then? How to form ideas? Paper was good. Thoughts were scrambled and threaded with premature and delicately wrapped guilts. Childlike in their language, its expression, but heftier in weight in subject matter. Small letters of apology or forgiveness were written to various adults with whom I was too scared to interact. Deep, young guilt. Sorry that I didn't respond to them, forgiving them for making me nervous. These letters were locked inside a small box. Only ever read later, by my older self.

Sitting on the dark-green carpeted stairs in a bright-red school uniform, peering between worn wooden banister poles, I watched something monstrous. Uncanny. Familiar and yet not. The face of my older sister, Kerrie, growing puce, aggressive, spewing out anger much bigger than I had ever seen before. Bigger again than Kerrie. A small, delicate fourteen-year-old face with a nose piercing that healed wrong because she got it done the weekend before she visited our cousin, then rode one of their bikes with no brakes down a hill and used her foot to brake instead. Dropping off a loose runner and dragging the top of her foot fast down a steep hill peeling back skin and flesh and dotting the blood wound with pebbles and dirt. An entire strip on the top of her foot was exposed and, in my muddled recollection, forewent any healing. The nose piercing from the weekend previous had somehow demanded all the healing energy in the body. Any healing properties went straight to her soft teenage nose such that her foot became more infected with each day. No skin weaving over, knitting together. Just raw pus and wound. The body, it seemed, produced enough 'healing properties' because the nose ring 'over-healed'. Skin, in fact, grew on top of it. Swallowed the little diamond. So here I was, face pressed between the wooden banisters, staring at the skin-covered lump of diamond in the nose of my sister's red, angry face. I was so close I could've reached out and touched her. I was on a high step so was eye to eye with her for once. With the stretch of her teenage face, at once young and old in different scowls.

She was screaming at our father. I can't remember what she was saying. But I can remember that he was screaming back. Each with everything they had. Him, obviously, having more. My sister's teenage voice breaking and rasping in the face of his deep boom. It was quite obviously unfair, even to my young self. An unequal match. Perhaps because of this, I remembered only what he said. Not because he was louder and therefore more important or his words more memorable. But because of some core instinct that no matter what my sister screamed at him, the extra bulb of flesh on the side of her young nose, which was constantly twitching out of nerves, the string of friendship bracelets on her arm and the purple glittered nail polish on her fingernails levelled any possibility of guilt. She was only taking on his original anger and reshaping it as quickly as she could to send it back. Where else would she have got it? Anything she said that was bad was him. Came from him. And so I thought at the time that he must be the real and only monster. I didn't take the time to imagine him as a teenager or child nursing a cold or a grazed knee, fighting with a father, being a brother, though I am sure all of these things happened. I didn't have the space to imagine it. Perhaps if I had a moment to unflinch, my mind could've carried itself to meet a version of him with which I could sympathise. Maybe it is yet to happen. The other day I poured a glass of milk and remembered something good about my Dad. He used to pour a glass of milk from a height every time. There would always be a lid of white bubbles. Maybe I am yet to find him somewhere in my mind doing other plain harmless funny things.

The familiar part of the uncanny was probably just my sister. Some strange reflection of his aggression – guiltless though. To look at him was infinitely harder. He was just beyond the door frame in the kitchen still. I was sitting on the stairs facing down to the front door, my sister was standing in the hallway, back to the front door, and he was in the kitchen, directly in my sister's line of sight. Of course, I could see parts of him on my sister's face. Not in it; not resemblance. On it. The particulars of his venom during that fight, each fight really, would pin themselves on my sister's facial expressions. She was taking them on. Balancing them on her face before she reordered them to give them back. The transition between absorption, assimilation and return showed slips of fear, slips of sadness, slips of a bottom lip. Seeing this from the stairs was scary. Made me even more reluctant to walk down the rest of the way, stand behind my sister and look at our dad. I could only see my sister. And only hear my dad. The words were bad, the name-calling. But anger meeting anger was a safe space. It was when she was having those slips and he caught them and he commented on them that things got really bad. That he got a taste for some weakness or vulnerability in her. He would laugh then and I would retreat up the stairs. There was something maniacal in his laugh that let us know, calling out to us like a warning, a siren that said, 'I will really lose control now.' Laughing was scarier than screaming. Screaming was controlled.

Parcel Out the Body

WHEN PHIL WAS LIVING IN THE PSYCHIATRIC WARD IN HOSPITAL, OTHER PATIENTS WOULD BOW AS THEY PASSED HER. All types of people. The young skinhead who she thought liked me. The lady in her fifties from Kildare who got a belt of a horse in the head and developed a brain injury. She called my grandmother 'boss' and once told me, on my way to Phil's ward, that she was a great boss and she loved working for her. There was the red-haired man who was so gentle and kind – Phil used to get annoyed, saying he fancied her.

He disputed this but still felt the need to give her a packet of Tayto cheese and onion crisps and a twenty euro note at least twice a week. He bowed too. And brought her water from the cooler. There was only one man who didn't bow to her. He looked like the dad in *The Royle Family*. His simple lack of subservience bothered her to the point of stealing sandwiches. She watched nurses cater to the needs of his diabetes, which might mean snacks or meals outside of set hours like the rest of them. She would eavesdrop on his sandwich order, which was left in the fridge behind the nurses' station for him to request later. As soon as the nurses shift changed, Phil would request the sandwich from a new nurse with every ingredient detailed. She ate them for a week and then began just binning them. When they fought over the remote in the TV room she poured boiling water all over his lap. She was dangerous. You had to be aware of that.

My visiting naturally develops into my attendance at a performance of hers. Phil has a series of songs, each day, to which God has ascribed special meaning, special meaning for the two of them alone. Her favourite nurse prints out the lyrics for Phil on days we can't visit and she pores over them, finding God's meaning and responding. When I arrive, she leans against the wall beside her bed, the small of her back pressing her hands flat against the wall and begins. She is singing 'Down by the Salley Gardens'. She sings every word with her own version of heart-breaking intonation. She seems to know the ache it was written with, and is reminded of it now as she sings. I am entranced until she removes her right arm from behind her back and gives the middle finger to a young patient passing by. This other patient is about my age. Phil keeps singing, doesn't falter even momentarily, still smiling and still holding her middle finger up, carrying it sideways across her chest, arm outstretched, to follow the woman out of the room. I smile at the woman, who tentatively smiles back. She seems to know there is a risk involved in reaching out in any direction Phil doesn't want her to. Phil drops and extends her jaw, exposing the full bottom row of teeth and in a threatening jolt, lunges towards the woman, still singing. She retreats when the woman has passed, rolling her 'r's – 'in a field down by the r-r-river' – in unison with John McCormack, who sings from the iPhone in my apologetic, waving hand.

She returns, full performance. It is hard to re-enter with her but you can stand outside it and watch. Something in my heart is held and sinking at once. I stay with her and listen more. Sometimes I have to steer the conversation away from certain topics that are so outright abusive that to sit and listen is to be complicit. The end scale of her terrorising is particularly venomous. She says that God tells her to do the hurtful things she does to people, so she does them. It doesn't take long for these events to dissipate, for the bad taste of her bullying to fade. This is because I am bearing witness to the sheer weight of living there. It costs her so much. It costs all of them so much. The woman who was on the receiving end of Phil's threat just clawed at the cheek of another patient in the hallway. My position by Phil's bed lets me see the moving edge of the commotion and hear its full echo and shriek, layered over Phil's oper-atic interpretation of the song. I place my iPhone on the bed, and John McCormack continues to lead their duet. The iPhone and the sterile hospital bed it rests on push in their own way against Phil's age, her belongings, their smell, her choice of artist. Institution and home pass through each other like ghosts. Old music passes through new technology. There is a weird cycle to it all, and justification.

Everything, slightly uncomfortable, feels right. None of the bad things are okay, but there is so little goodness you have to stare at it in case it disappears, *until* it does. Give it your undivided attention. Play 'Macushla' next without her asking. Don't let the near-setting sun peeking down below the open blind be a prompt to go home. The wind lightly taps the blind off the frame of the open window. Watch the flicker of white light that bounces up to her chin and back to her neck as she stands, singing. Watch it then pour over her whole face as she slumps into her chair and starts the next song, veering into 'Macushla'. Her face now featureless in a glowing white light. Notice it on her, the light flattening her face, cancelling any of the features that jut out towards you, like her nose or high cheekbones, but not quite reaching her deep-set eyes. Don't mope, but do let in the feeling that you love this face; that you love watching the light pouring over it eclipse its years. Stay longer again when five more songs have passed and you would be well expected to jangle your keys. Get tea then or hot chocolate, yes hot chocolate, from the cafe upstairs. Say you'll be back in a minute and come back in a minute. Give her as many experiences in there, not only of you being in there too, but you being on your way back. In there and elsewhere, returning momentarily. Give her whatever fleeting comfort might be provided in expecting to see your face around the corner in a minute and then actually seeing it. Ask her what else she'd like to sing after she has had half of her hot chocolate and said, 'This is such a treat.' Stay till dusk comes and goes and the sky is navy and colder than was the sharp afternoon blue. Don't think too long about the fact that you could happily take a cushion and stay the night. Think even less about how this particular day you feel paralysed at the prospect of walking out and leaving her there. Just of leaving – don't think of that. Maintain the sugar coma you've sunk into with her so you can leave numb, without thinking about where you are, where you were, where she still is, or that with every traffic light and gear change you're getting further away from that. Most days it is not a good idea to think about it but while you are leaving it is absolutely forbidden. You have forbidden yourself access to that thought. It would collapse the entire act. Avoid eye contact with yourself in the lift mirror on the way out. Your phone has no reception in the lift but still, tap your passcode in and swipe the screens around until you reach the reception level and can escape whatever you look like when you leave your grandmother in a psychiatric ward alone. You don't want to know what you look like when you do that.

Each time she sings 'Macushla' it feels like something is being summed up. It feels like something, usually strewn across generations, is being packaged and wrapped. Not love itself, but the act of loving something unloved to date. Perhaps it is arms reaching through the years, enfolding and binding me, that I feel through her voice. Something in her voice sounds like it has been there longer than she has been here singing. I don't exactly feel closer to her as she sings, but closer, through her, to someone else. To her own mother and hers before. Macushla's lips say death is a dream. Phil seems to be dreaming of that recently, and I am dreaming through her voice, while it is still here, of the lives that bore us both. I feel an acute pressure in the window of this voice closing. It is already just ajar now. The voice I hear in vain is already strained.

'Macushla' in Irish is *mo chuisle*: my pulse or vein; my pulsing heart. A term of endearment if one was to address you *a chuisle*: darling. Here, it is *mo chuisle*. Here, as she gives voice to our lineage, it is my pulse I feel. I feel the pulse of her blood in my veins as she sings. It calms me. I can't always place the softness, the sadness. I could place it with history perhaps, but that placement is so often stripped of feeling. This softness and sadness overwhelm where dates on pages can only inform. It is stronger than psychiatric family history that tries to explain everything away. I am sick of things being hidden. Something deep and internal feels bruised or darkened. Almost damp but not quite, and more unsettling for that uncertainty. I think of the smattering of veins under her old skin. They still encase her blood, which still flows. The flowing blood still encompasses something of me and something of others before me. But that something is already fragmented and scattering. I look at the skin of her hands and think of the bruised apples she cooked with when I was a child. And then I think of her mother's hands and how I don't know them and how I haven't touched them. I think of the skin of her mother's hands, hard or cracked maybe from all the movements of washing and dressing and cleaning the babies that became my elders. I think of Phil's throat. Of the sound that rises it in and how it fractures my understanding of time, how it gives voice to a temporal shock of sorts. Sings its own trauma and someone else's like an old baby wailing and laughing at once. Summoning lineage as she sings. There is something that feels like deep time that quivers in Phil's throat sometimes. Something that feels ancestral.

*

When I was about fourteen, Phil's younger sister, Vera, died. At the funeral, Vera's childhood friend walked up to me and began sobbing. She told my mother I looked exactly like Vera as a teenager. Exactly as she had remembered her. I had seen photos and thought the resemblance was remote at best but nonetheless found myself standing a little taller, my feet rooted a little sturdier, after the comment.

Any work that I have seen meditating on family likeness and resemblance always holds me a little longer. When I first encountered Tom Wood's exhibition *Mothers, Daughters, Sisters* at the Arles photography festival, the faces seemed sometimes like puzzles to be figured out. The resemblance was not always immediately apparent. My favourite image is of a young child in her mother's arms. The top of the mother's head is cut off by the frame and you can only see her nose and lips. That is all you need to see. The curve of her nose and philtrum is replicated mere inches below the original, in miniature form, clinging to her chest.

My mother is always quick to spot the similar features in family members. I have my grandfather's forehead lines when I raise my eyebrows. I have my uncle's eyes when I am speaking passionately about something. My mother seats all of these identities in mine. Finds a way for me to keep them. I have the face of my grandmother and her sister when it is relaxed. And I have their mother's side profile. She seems to see the man in me when I am animated. The woman when I rest.

Around the time of Vera's funeral, my mother lingered on this idea of me looking like her. Of my face comprising some maternal lineage. She had me pose in an aisle of accessories in New Look, wearing a brown bucket hat and huge sunglasses, head tilted slightly to the left, trying to match an old family photo she had in mind. She rooted it out when we got home and held it up to the image of me on her phone. Behind me in the photo is a teenage boy in a soft-grey tracksuit. He has four or five paper shopping bags hanging on his forearm and is sucking on the straw of a McDonald's cup. His mother is rifling through racks of clothes, frowning. I look both uncomfortable and like I am trying extremely hard all at once. While she sees the resemblance, all I can see is the McDonald's cup. All I can imagine is the greasy meal in that boy's stomach. Piles of clothes stacked in that mother's bedroom as she searches for more.

In *Camera Lucida,* Roland Barthes designates 'the genetic feature, the fragment of oneself or of a relative which comes from some ancestor' as more penetrating than mere likeness. 'The Photograph gives a little truth, on condition that it parcels out the body. But this truth is not that of the individual, who remains irreducible, it is the truth of lineage.' This thought is initially comforting because it makes my life or Phil's life or my mother's life, when standing alone, seem somehow immutable. But it is also comforting because these individual impermanences, when combined, create something. The individual and immutable body is parcelled out on the understanding that lineage will restore some broader, longer, deeper truth. I know I have the same shaped lips as Phil because our half-used lipsticks look the same. The curve is similarly pronounced. I can carve my closeness to her into a small cosmetic stick. It reminds me that everything I come in contact with can be marked at once by our dual touch. It is more penetrating than mere likeness.

*

In early 2017, Phil agreed to have a mastectomy to prove a point: that she didn't have cancer and, furthermore, that the body she was in wasn't hers. She was living at home at the time and we spent the evening before the surgery in her sitting room, sipping two glasses of sherry. There was often an opposition of sorts between the doctors and us. When they commented upon Phil's youthful presentation, we responded uniformly with tight-lipped smiles, implying it is with no thanks to Western medicine that she looks, and usually feels, so good. After the surgery I came back to visit her. I remember driving back during rush hour and seeing boys from posh schools weave between the wet traffic on their bikes, skidding into the entrances of their large homes. I wondered what people they were. I wondered which spare rooms student doctors rented in their houses. How long it took before acting a certain way meant they were a certain way.

When I walked into her private room on the ward, Phil was wearing turquoise pyjamas with yellow and deep purple flowers on them, and a matching light dressing gown. She was slightly flushed from the whole ordeal and the general heat on the ward. Her rosy cheeks, youthful, sparked a sadness in me that I didn't even notice until I woke at home the next morning and thought back to them. Though I wouldn't usually, wouldn't ever, I was catering to her like an invalid. In this week, these hours at least, she was. She rummaged through the bag of things I'd brought her, rubbing cream onto her face while I watched the fold of her pyjama top for a new shadow. I was still lingering on the infancy of my thoughts from the evening before the surgery. Once her bag was packed for the hospital stay and we had arranged a time to leave the house to beat the traffic, I slipped into thinking about the fact that some of her body would be gone by that time tomorrow. I felt suddenly possessive, clouded with anger. I don't know why but I was upset not to know where it would go. I didn't want to ask anyone and I didn't really want to know, but I was angry nonetheless, that some essential part of her was about to become displaced. Not technically essential but adjacent. Essential not only in the obvious ways, the early years of latch and suck for my mother and uncles, but the years that followed as a pillow, a familiar place for those young heads to rest again after she had been away. A shape that held when everything else warped and bent – time, memories, safety, warmth.

Phil's mother had breast cancer too. As a patient in Grangegorman Mental Hospital, her breast cancer and perceived madness were always intertwined in stories I was told. In most family photographs I have seen of her, she always seems more physically incapacitated than others. Although all subjects are frozen in the image, I can imagine the movements of others before and after the frame was captured. She is always rooted. She is always sitting. It is not residential in the stately sense, or even necessarily maternal. She sits in chairs that seem flimsy. In one photograph she is resting in a light fold-up sun chair that looks like it could collapse if her weight weren't so inconsequential. Her eyes are shaded so I cannot tell if they are open or closed, when they might open or close again. I cannot even meet her in her image. In another, she sits gangly and out of place in a baby's buggy, looking down to the left while Phil stands on her right-hand side, roughly two or three years old, and looks straight into the camera, chin lifted and one eye closed. Whether she is winking or squinting it is unclear but either way, I know her closed eye will open again, the open eye will close, the mischievous sucked-in bottom lip will fall back into place, will grow into the aged shape I've come to know.

After the mastectomy I stayed into the evening, settled into the armchair beside her hospital bed. We enjoyed some mindless TV together now that we were no longer occupied with concern for this imminent procedure. I handed her her tea every couple of minutes on request. She was propped up but leaning back in her bed. Slight pain with moving and general discomfort had kicked in as the long day took its toll and the stronger pain relief naturally wore off. She reached out for some grapes, which she had dismissed earlier. As I washed the grapes over the sink, with my back turned to her, I commented on how good she looked after such a day.

When I turned back around she had whipped back the blanket to reveal the turquoise outfit again, crossed her legs at a slight bend with her toes delicately pointed, and said, 'Feed them to me from above.'

I hesitated.

'Like a Roman patrician,' she gestured, one elbow propping her fresh torso up on the bed, the other flailing above her head, fingers pointing down in an animated attempt at holding a bunch of invisible grapes.

I understood the aesthetic she was going for. Anticipating the mortification of having to explain what was about to ensue, I closed the door over and complied. We watched the news about the Fort Lauderdale shooting, not pausing our Roman scene to acknowledge the newsreader's sweeping statement about the shooter's mental-health history, with that jarring tone of justification. My clouded anger had settled. Nothing essential seemed lost now that we were on the other side of the event. No breast tissue or lip curve, no wrinkled forehead or side profile was truly individual and so could never be lost. All features comprise some longer historical exposure. All can be retold in the image of new bodies. Each set in their own way. Each parcelled out for a moment, before being recalled to take their place in the longer truth of lineage.

MK 277.5

MK 277.5 IS THE PLOT NUMBER OF MY GREAT-
GRANDMOTHER'S GRAVE. I have been so consumed
by tracing ideas of her – records of her life when
it was being lived, records of atrocities when
they were being done to her, records of her image
when it was captured, records of the place she
called home when it was the site of brutal experi-
mental abuse – that it slipped my mind entirely to
trace the record of the last place her body went.
It was a windy afternoon in the third week of
September when I entered Glasnevin Cemetery.

I was greeted, in the order that follows, by a red-and-white security gate for parking, a man in a small purpose-built cabin to welcome and direct people, and Roger Casement's grave. All three, spilling back, were the first things I could see. As we drove around to the car park on the left, my mother commented on the man's trousers – confused still to be met with empty silence, as she has been for years now, when she throws out thoughtless jabs at people she drives past for the benefit of my sister and me who never, in fact, benefit from these running commentaries. She runs to the toilet when we arrive.

I approach the man. I ask about finding a grave number. I am halfway through my sentence when I realise he is eating his lunch. I apologise while he waves his hand at me, with a scrunched-up tissue in it, mouth full and smiling: no, no, he gestures. He swallows then speaks. 'Okay so, we'll need the full name, the age at death and the location of death to get you started,' he says. Brigid Duff, aged forty, Grangegorman Mental Hospital, are the answers. I don't say this. He has already moved on to writing a name and number on a page for me. 'Call Lynn, who runs the genealogy research and is now working from home. Give her those three details and she should be able to help. She might be on her lunch too for another ten minutes though.'

I call and leave a message, my name and number. I move closer to the museum and cafe building and wait on a bench. Lynn returns my call and I am crouched now, by a tree nearby, trying to block my body from the wind so I can say clearly down the phone, 'Brigid Duff, died aged forty, in Grangegorman Mental Hospital,' my back to Casement's bones. I can hear her typing and then she calls out to me: 'MK 277.5, St Brigid's Section.' I thank her, hang up and turn my back on the tree I have been crouched in front of to find my mother approaching the man in his cabin still eating his lunch. She is walking briskly and I am already protective of him, of his lunch hour, of his trousers. I walk-run to her waving my phone in the air trying to communicate across the wind and courtyard that I have it.

I begin to follow the St Brigid's arrow, passing the cabin again, and he calls out to me, 'Did you get it? C'mere let me see.' I turn back to him.

Somehow my awareness of this man's lunch hour makes everything feel time-sensitive. I start to run again, towards him. I think I have everything under control but really, if anyone was watching from the cafe, I have been running back and forth past Roger Casement's grave for the past ten minutes, waving my phone at people. He tells me I'll need to look for the red painted mark of MK on the far wall as I walk along St Brigid's section. As *soon* as I see that, he tells me, I need to turn immediately to the right and follow that row of graves. Some will have MK stamps on the back or front, followed by their number, so I will know when I'm getting close. He warns me that there might not even be a headstone. I might just find the rough area, the small section of land that holds her. He wishes me luck in a way that I have never been wished luck before. It is more jovial than you might expect for a graveyard and I don't know what exactly about it made me feel so happy. A sense of purpose and weirdly, perhaps, a sense of propriety. That it was my grave to find.

*

I walk for a while. When I googled it earlier, Wikipedia told me that 1.5 million people were interred here. I continue along her line of graves, which is nowhere near a path, even of grass, on either side so I have to walk over graves. I do it delicately at first, as if that will make a difference. As if these haphazard rows of dry grass and old stones are thin, watery sheets of ice. After a while I walk less delicately. Not only do I not have time for it but my body aches a little with its increasingly poor attempt at a respectful grave-hopping gait. I walk normally for a while and then, selfishly in hindsight, stride with a harsher footfall. The melancholy air has dissipated into a gentle chase. I am searching gravestones for MK followed by three specific numbers. I pass MK 36, MK 132, MK 188. I am dismissing everything else about these headstones. I am not reading names, or ages, or years. I am not looking at photos or fake plants or flowers. MK 207. Again, I am almost running. The man at the entrance has finished his lunch and Brigid has been buried here for seventy-five years. I am almost breaking into a sprint as I push into the 250s of MK.

I find the area. Have walked past her number and so take myself back. I think I am being meticulous and looking at everything but I cannot find it. My mother catches up with me after a while. I wonder if she broke out into a run at any point, behind me. If she were chasing me back into our history through a graveyard. I find it, eventually. Had been circling it for a few minutes.

There is a headstone. It is white marble and curves down on one side, almost making a little slide of the smooth old stone. There are flecks and lined traces of grey. The headstone reads:

In Loving Memory
of
Our Parents Brigid Duff (Cissie)
who died 6-10-1946
and
Mick Duff (Ga-Ga)
who died 5-11-1994

Immediately I learn that I have been spelling Cissie wrong. I have been spelling it 'Sissy'. I have always liked the name, and haven't minded its spelling but now realise I have committed to print elsewhere a typed suggestion of her as cowardly. Cissie is much harder, more robust. The C protecting what follows, cushioning it in under its capital wing. Next I see that the black ink of these engraved words is completely rubbed out now on 'Brigid'. Her first name is see-through. The only other word that is equally transparent is 'who', her 'who'. Three words on this headstone refer to her existence. I have been butchering one and the other two are empty here. 'Parents' still has ink, which of course alludes to her too. Although only 'Pa' is fully coloured in, 'rents' has faded considerably.

I have traced my way carefully, if frantically, here to her grave. When I found the red painted MK on the wall I saw only that, turned immediately to the right, as I was told to. As I trace my steps back with my mother, we approach the red letters again and she points beyond them, through the bars of the graveyard railing, to a Mormon church across the road. It is almost directly aligned with Cissie's row number. Immediately, it is a landmark for future visits. It is also the church she used to go to, every week for years, she tells me. The church where she used to give up one-third of her pocket money. The church, one of many, where Phil was looking for something. Phil was always looking for something in churches, my mam said. Every week Phil took my mam to the church right across the road from the exact row of graves that held their mother, grandmother and still, now, I am told this like it is mere coincidence.

God or Some Other Soothing Opiate

'STILL, AS WE MATURE INTO OUR MORTALITY, WE
BEGIN TO GINGERLY DIP OUR HORROR-TINGLING
TOES INTO THE VOID, HOPING THAT OUR MIND
WILL SOMEHOW EASE ITSELF INTO DYING, THAT
GOD OR SOME OTHER SOOTHING OPIATE WILL
REMAIN AVAILABLE AS WE VENTURE INTO THE
DARKNESS OF NON-BEING.'

Aleksandar Hemon

The 7up bubbles around Phil's parched lips. She is undernourished and filled instead with sugar. Sedate. I sit in her room and listen to her describe the ways in which she avoids taking her tablets. The specific gymnastics of her tongue, pink and protective. I am not moved to respond. I am not upset that she is not taking them. I cannot say with confidence that she should be taking these tablets.

The topic, in general, feels precarious. Thin ice over a cold void. I should move delicately. I should move. I am standing still but the ice will crack soon. I must speak about it even though it is difficult. Even though I am confused. Who am I to question medical advice, I ask myself. The voice is never mine when I ask this question but it nonetheless comes from inside me. I never answer it. Perhaps if I just move, for now, towards the questions. Let answers come later. From elsewhere. My questions; or rather, one question. One question that grows. Grows legs, climbs to its feet, stumbles then suddenly runs; no amble, no gentle saunter. A sprint. Running for its life. My question is running for its life. Putting distance between itself and the object of its concern. What will we call that object? The tablets? No, they are a vehicle. A tool. The object is the institution. The institution *as object*. Let us look at it that way. Let us switch the narrative, if we can. Let us mark and stamp and label *that* place. Fix *it* within rigid parameters. Let us run. One question grows and then mutates, bouncing on to the back of a new form.

Why is she being medicated?

Why is she being medicated against her will?

Why is she being medicated against her will in a way that leaves her drowsy, limp?

Where has this drowsy, sedated woman put my strong-willed grandmother?

*

There was a sense of achievement, as a child, when the doctor put you on an antibiotic. A sense that your mother's money hadn't been wasted, a sense that her instinct was right to bring you. A sense of validation. If the prescription also included steroids or an A&E referral *just in case,* validation would turn to guilt. A fine line. Ten days to two weeks of antibiotics was the sweet spot. You would be happy for your mother for getting it right. She would feel bad for you, poor thing. Just bad enough that she could manage, that you both could. You weren't sick enough to scare her yet, for her to freeze in the face of it. For her to ask how you are feeling and then interrupt your honest response with, 'Ah, Molly, I hate hearing that. Ah Jesus, don't say that.' Two days off school, two weeks of medicine and one free-for-all trip to Tesco. Tesco was a different landscape when your prescription was sitting in a plastic basket behind the counter in the chemist next door. There was never the sense that the fever, the spasms, the pain, was your body doing the work, responding to something. That it was trying to tell you something you should hear. Just something they should quieten, shush, cool, still. And that you should let them. Always let them do what they think is right for your body.

*

The question of chemical incarceration is also a question about family. The question of psychiatric incarceration in Ireland is already inherently a question of family. In *Negotiating Insanity in the Southeast of Ireland, 1820–1900*, Catherine Cox describes the Irish family dynamic as being devoid of 'emotional gratification'. Cox goes on to explore the family as a site of emotional tension – ranging from affection and support to violence, discord and stress. She explores the interactions between 'local protagonists' and the Irish asylum system. I paused at the phrase 'local protagonists'. It felt familiar. I have been a part of Phil's involuntary incarcerations.

I remember meeting the inexperienced locum who parked around the corner from Phil's house. She acted as if she were worried about being seen or caught. As if Phil would be on high alert. She was like the type of diligent child who kept herself so busy she forgot to stop being a diligent child when she grew up. She pulled up in a bright red Audi and looked terrified. She didn't get out of the car to speak to me although we both knew I had to give her a crash course on the past year of Phil's mental health. So from the kerb I found myself bending down to her window; then, to save my back, leaning onto it with both forearms; then crouching down on my hunkers and lengthening my neck so our eyes could meet; then standing up and leaning on the roof of her car while I spoke, sacrificing eye contact for the sake of my strained back. I reassured her I just needed a house visit review from a GP on the proposed day of 'the move'. I just needed to get her in the door long enough for them to speak so that she could pass professional comment on Phil's mental state. She picked relentlessly at a spot on her milky white chest while I spoke and a small red dot of blood sat there when she'd finished, matching her car perfectly. She still didn't move.

I guessed from her frantic eyes and the fact that she hadn't even taken her seatbelt off yet that if she wasn't such a stickler for rules her whole life she might've written the review without even seeing Phil. It angered me that someone like this was seconds away from pathologising my grandmother. And yet, I was the one bringing her to Phil. I was tightly woven into the process of incarceration – I was as much to blame. I carried a mixture of love and concern in me that this woman did not possess, but still I was equally at fault. On another occasion when I was younger still, a teenager, I was sent in first, to prise the door open. I sat with Phil for about fifteen minutes, having tea, knowing that my mother, two policemen and one doctor were outside in their cars and would knock at the door any minute. That small window of time, that blurry moment, void of sound, of smell, of any sense at all, comprises in its exact senselessness the pinnacle of my guilt.

*

In *Asylums, Families and the State*, discussing the late 1800s, Mark Finnane examines the interplay between family and State in admitting people to the asylum system by reminding us that, while the State defined the contours of the institutions, the institutions themselves were 'moulded by the perceptions and actions of the populations they served'. I still believe this to be true. Something about my role in those interactions was akin to sculpture. I helped to shape the narrative clay, warped and uneven as it was, before it was fired in the kiln. I can see this now but the ceramic is hardened. I cannot remould it without smashing the whole thing. I can put her into a hospital but I cannot take her out.

In Gleann na nGealt, the Valley of the Mad, in West Kerry, there is a well that people flock to. They visit because it is believed to improve conditions of mental illness. Scientists have taken samples of the well water and found it had high levels of lithium. Phil has always taken seriously the advice to drink at least two litres of water a day while on lithium. Six packs of Evian water bottles almost served as a rite of passage, an entry ticket when I would visit her in hospital some years ago. She drinks so much water that she is not as limp and gasping as others, and by association perhaps not as damaged. Hydrated, engaged, capable still. I can see the lift in her in the space of a few minutes when she has had some water, like a high-speed video of a plant being watered. Visiting Phil in mid-July it is hot and she needs extra water. Her water is thickened with powder now, made gelatinous and gloopy so that she won't choke. Still she drinks fast. She can hold the cup herself again. Her fingers bend in different ways to make this happen. Bending in on themselves like they have been melted by the hot July sun. Somehow, it is still glamorous. There is a heatwave and her room is stuffy even with the windows opened to their widest latch. She is wearing two tops and I take one off for her. I wonder if I will hurt her, if I will need help to lift her body forward to remove it.

We work together instead. She can prop herself forward enough in the wheelchair for me to peel the orange cotton top from her heavy white T-shirt underneath. Her entire back is damp. I pull the white T-shirt from her skin repeatedly, airing out the space between her back and top. Henri-Cartier Bresson said that photography was like getting between the skin and shirt of the subject. Her grey hair is long and I twist it up into a loose bun without bobbins or clips. Nothing to pull at her. I offer her a cool cloth for her neck. Her tired eyes widen a little as she assents. I search through her drawers for a face cloth, a small towel, something suitable. I have moved her wheelchair to look out the window and now she is positioned directly in front of the armchair I sit in. Then her nurse comes in and Phil and I are sitting beside her bed, facing each other as her bun comes undone and her hair flaps down onto the bright blue-and-white J Cloth I have folded into a strip and wrapped around the back of her neck. There is something comical about our scene. She smirks first. I follow.

A little later, after describing how difficult her life has become, Phil tells me to get the nurse. She is agitated. When he arrives and asks what he can do, she touches her chest and says there is pain. 'You have chest pain?' he asks. 'Yes.' 'Okay, I can get you something for that, no problem. I will be back in a minute.' When he leaves I ask if it is chest pain or heartache and she says heartache. He returns with a raspberry flavoured Petits Filous yoghurt that has crushed-up painkillers in it. He feeds it to her, wiping the codeine-flecked dairy from her bottom lip with the spoon. She trusts him. I am at a remove of the kind that will help me sleep later. Their relationship is strong. 'I hope I'm not a burden,' she says, and he says, 'Yes, yes it is burning in here today.' I see that she has the full picture while he does not. I can tell that she heard the word 'burning' clearly. That she knows he didn't say, 'Yes you are a burden.' She smiles up at him as he scrapes the last of the yoghurt with the spoon and I can see that the care is reciprocal. She finishes the yoghurt and he leaves and I say, 'Petits Filous for the heartache,' and she smiles at me and closes her eyes.

*

In the *New Yorker*, Lou Stoppard writes about hospital art. Tracing the intention and value of nature art to the topography of wellness, Stoppard wonders how a sick person's environment should be defined. She talks about nature art being therapeutic or calming for those with certain illnesses, but perhaps jarring or triggering for others. She touches on Ben Lerner's contention that the suggestion of art alone is what is truly required in these spaces.

Phil does not think of herself as sick. The space that she occupies does not come across as a sick person's environment. There is no suggestion of art in this space either, at least not on the walls. The suggestion of art is a bodily phenomenon where Phil lives, proposed through fashion or facial expressions. It is not two-dimensional. It cannot be hung up on a wall, suspended. Any possible suggestions of art on her hospital walls, now that I think of them, propose an infancy that is out of touch. There is a sign on the door to Phil's bedroom. It has only bright primary colours. It has only rounded shapes, rounded letters; no corners, nothing sharp. Her name is typed in bold Comic Sans, at an exceptionally large print size – the sign reads 'Phyllis's Room'. Beside this rounded writing is a rounded cartoon image of a chair. The sign is laminated. The lamination is rounded. All the other doors here sport an exact replica. The chair is the same. The colours are the same. Only the name is different.

Inside her room, beside the door, is a printed neuropsychology file note slipped into a clear plastic poly-pocket and taped to the wall. It includes a list of thirteen recommendations for responding to Phil when she is distressed or anxious. They are detailed. They are specific to Phil. They include calming phrases that she likes. Various points on the list, expanded upon respectively in clinical language, can be summarised as pertaining to respect. Reading through the entire list I can see her. Her character, somehow, is reflected here in this mindful guide. It is also printed in Comic Sans. The very last point on the list I reread as she sleeps in her chair behind me. 'Avoid discussing her personal history unless she raises it; this can be a trigger for distress for Phyllis.' Knowing the details of this distressing personal history, living some of it with her and agreeing that discussing it with her would be triggering, I came to understand something. Phil is still here, still speaking, still herself but the vast majority of her lived experience to date is no longer on the table. On an instinctual level I already knew this. We never bring old things up. Why would we? It would serve no purpose. But seeing it here, printed on her wall, in the quiet of her slumber that mirrors this vast emptiness, this instinctive and now insisted-upon silence gives me pause. While I cannot claim to know the contours of her personal history I can gather the parts I am familiar with. I can tell people why they are important. I can embody my lineage in a way that is not attempting to represent a certain struggle, or speak on anyone's behalf but that sits adjacent to the through-line of suffering I have witnessed, the tenor of our history.

*

Back when Phil lived in the old hospital, we offered to bring in photographs, or paintings, things she might like to hang on the wall or put on her bedside locker. The clarity and intention of her refusal was striking. Images somehow represented a boundary she was not willing to cross. On her side of that boundary, the hospital space she inhabited was still exceptionally homely. I recall one visit in particular. Arriving into her basement ward, it smelled of stale cigarettes. It was freezing until I passed an unsettling burst of warmth halfway down the corridor. The atmosphere was largely unwelcoming until I saw her. She wore a navy jumper with pink and yellow flowers and stood at the end of the corridor waiting for me. When I reached her, she offered me freshly squeezed orange juice. The juice never appeared but the home-making was in the offer. The bodily inhabitation of a suggestion of art. A suggestion of the art of home-making. A suggestion of the art of home-making within the confines of involuntary incarceration. Around this time, Phil was still refusing medication.

When I interact, as a family member, with the carceral institution as it functions today, everything is washed with kindness, with care. I know Phil's favourite nurse. I smile at her. My complicity in the process of incarceration is embodied in the softness of my interactions with its caretakers. This softness complicates my grip on guilt. It feels essential that I do not let go of that guilt. So much is yet to be done. I cannot slip into the softness of these interactions, into the bat of the false eyelashes on Phil's favourite nurse. A woman whose eyelashes I am aware of only because Phil calls me over as that nurse is fixing her trousers and says, 'Aren't her eyelashes gorgeous?' 'Yes!' I exclaim, a mere four eyelashes to my name, across both eyes, both lids.

There is charm and humour and real care in these spaces.

Still I am uneasy. I am worried about institutional lineage. I cannot dismiss the particular history of these institutions as merely a disavowed inheritance – something lingers, not hidden perhaps, but unseen and under-acknowledged nonetheless. I am trying to recognise the shades of this. I am concerned knowing that the psychiatric institution today is a descendant of Grangegorman's botched lobotomies and insulin-induced comas. If the present-day institution is my counterpart in this lineage, why isn't it doing the same work? Where is the national apology? The recognition of mass torture and death? Why is the site of my great-grandmother's death in Grangegorman now a new college campus slabbed with fresh concrete? As I trace my own maternal lineage and find pockets of it warm and encouraging, others difficult and jarring, I operate from a place of fear knowing that the present-day psychiatric institution is not engaging in its equivalent lineal deep dive.

*

One month after Phil complained of heartache or chest pain she had a heart attack. She also contracted Covid at the same time. Doctors asked my mother and uncle about resuscitation. The very act of the question being posed gave us a suggestion. A suggestion of death hung on the walls of the apartment I was staying in, my mother's house in Liverpool, my uncle's in Donegal. Words I remember my mother saying to me on the phone that day include: cremation, poems, humanist, tired, ready. It wasn't the first time we'd had a conversation with words like these doing the heavy lifting. Less than a week later, Phil was eating food, strengthening up and was transferred back home to the psychiatric hospital and moved into an isolation ward for the remainder of her time with Covid. She was doing well, considering. Even as we celebrated the dizzying heights of that joy, the incident revealed the distance of the fall that would some day come. Must some day come. Kristeva writes, 'On account of the meaning maintained during the fading away period, there is an infinite possibility of ambivalent, polyvalent resurrections.' I know this is true for

Phil. These sporadic resurrections populating her late eighties. The meaning of her life is somehow neatly crystallised each time, concentrated down like a serum. We wash ourselves with it and go again. We take her lead.

A Location
That Resists Telling

PHIL WAS TAKEN TO TALLAGHT HOSPITAL BY AMBULANCE BECAUSE OF A CONSTANTLY DILATED PUPIL. We were told that possible causes for this could be a stroke, a brain bleed, or a tumour pressing on a nerve of the eye. There were no palatable options. She was also shaking severely but that was being put down to the lithium. In hindsight, the shakes were too severe, stronger than I had seen in other patients. In the weeks running up to this, I had become accustomed to watching her shuffle around her room, unable to lift her feet but also unable to stop them moving. Constantly on the go.

'Do you think I'm up for it?' she asked me one summer afternoon when Rónán and I visited with our dog.

'I don't know. Your shaking has improved a lot in the last few days. You're able to sit for a lot longer now than you were even a week ago.'

'Am I?'

'Definitely, yeah.'

'Okay, do you think we should go?'

'If you think you'd like it, would you?'

'Oh, yes. I'd love it. I would love to go for a drive. Do you think I can?'

'I think we can try it. We can make it short, and come back whenever you say.'

'Okay, great.'

We drove up to the Dublin Mountains, a short distance from her new hospital. I sat in the back seat, watching the light that fell through the trees flash by Rónán's arm as he drove, then slip past my leg before disappearing. I watched him with Phil, telling her his news, asking how she felt. I thought of a few months previous when she escaped the unit, not making it further than the local post office and I told him and he said we were family and that we had to support her. I thought of how he said that, with no weight at all, and watched him now speaking with her, stealing glances at her, taking her for a drive on a sunny afternoon with Lyric FM soothing her in the background and, caught off guard, my love for him seemed to grow.

We pulled up to a stretch of road in the Dublin Mountains that is awkwardly popular. A place that is so removed, peering down over the city, but where you could still expect to see a colleague or old fling emerge from the car that pulls up and inevitably blocks your view. You are at peace up there, you are enjoying the fresh air but you are always subconsciously reading the cars that drive by, cross-referencing the make, model and colour with people in and out of your life. I am happy I don't know what type of car my father drives.

We pull up and there is nobody else there. Rónán takes the dog for a run a little way down the gentle slope of mountainside to our left. I climb through the middle of the car like a child and take his place in the driver's seat. She looks out her window at them, or maybe she is looking to the mountain beyond, or above to the sky, or the city lights and smoke to the right of her windowed picture. It feels, to me, like she is protected in this car. Like nothing is too extreme but she gets to see new things. To her, it may not have felt real. It may not have felt real to be at the top of a mountain looking over her city of eighty-six years when, for months, she has had the same view from her hospital window of pebble-dashed walls and rusted balconies and patio tiles with sprouting weeds. The mountains circle the hospital but the aspect of her various bedrooms over the years never demonstrated it. The hospital makes little use of the environment, except in the brochures, and in the conversation with family members considering the place.

With her song 'Don't Sleep in the Subway', Petula Clark coaxed Phil out of the pantry. She slept there in protest for her first night after transferring to this new psychiatric hospital. The musical build-up to the chorus is so smooth it first brings to mind gowns swishing across waxed ballroom floors, for which you naturally substitute flat, plastic-packed hospital slippers dragged along glitter-flecked hospital floors. Not even lifted, just slid constantly. Dragged. God told her, through Clark, *Don't sleep in the subway, darling, don't stand in the pouring rain … The night is long, forget your foolish pride, nothing's wrong, now you're beside me again.* She giggled, mouthing these words to me. She didn't have her teeth in at the time. The staff had lost them. Most people's cheeks sag and hollow when they don't have their teeth in. Hers, somehow seem more rounded. It was the apple of her cheek I realised, still so high, that held in place whether her mouth was full of teeth or gum. 'So that's what He told me: "You know I'm beside you, nothing *is* wrong. They're all shadows." The only thing I don't like about it, though, is I thought I'd have a view of the Wicklow Mountains.'

*

'I think I need to walk,' she said. I knew there would probably be a need for her to get out of the car and pace a little but I didn't expect it to be so blustery up there. I walked around to her passenger side, the door swinging open with the wind. I turned her to the side, readjusted her orange linen trousers, which had wound under her thighs in a twist and seemed to be squeezing, maybe even hurting her. Once she was facing out, I lifted her up to standing, with the plan to steady ourselves against the car door before making any moves. As soon as she rose to her feet, her shoulder-length grey hair flew directly vertical above her head. I couldn't hear anything in the wind and with our faces just touching I could see only the close details in hers change in a way that I knew, from a few steps back, would be working together to make a smile. Suddenly it felt remarkable that she was here. I knew we had driven her and would only be out of the car for a few seconds, a minute at most, but it felt like a triumph that she was standing at such a height. I wanted Rónán to see this. I couldn't turn to wave him over, my body still holding hers up. I couldn't call him, my face still pressed against her cheek and ear. I stole a quick glance back, expecting to see his figure dotted somewhere in the green distance. Instead, he was running towards us with his camera in hand, frantically snapping.

Her loose cheeks were more prone to jowling in the wind than any I'd seen before but it wasn't too much. It wasn't people hurtling at unnatural speed along a rollercoaster. It was a natural rush. Tears, just from wind, streamed back along her temples in a straight line, slipping into her ear canal that could hear nothing. Nothing needed to be said anyway. Everything was felt. I could feel her warm clammy skin drying and cooling in seconds. We walked four steps. The length of the car. We turned again and slowly walked back.

*

Each time I leave her ward I walk down two flights of stairs. Before descending, I am faced with a large rectangular window that shows a deep green scene of trees and mountains. I don't know why it is a stairway that lets me see this. I don't know why it is a stairway that patients in her ward are not allowed to use. I don't know what architects or planners are doing. One day

I posted an image of the window to my Instagram story before driving home and when I pulled into the driveway my mother had replied: 'speaks volumes Xx'.

I have started reading Thomas Mann's *The Magic Mountain* on my friend's recommendation. When I am only a handful of pages in, and reading about Hans Castorp's memory of his relationship with his grandfather, I underline a section that meditates on the formless and uncritical judgements he made as a child that 'persisted into later life, as the elements of a perfectly conscious memory-picture, which defied expression or analysis, but was nonetheless positive for all that'. The second half of the next sentence I mark too: 'the close family tie and essential intimacy which not infrequently leaps over an intervening generation'. Like twins, I think.

*

It wasn't long after the day in the mountains that Phil was admitted to Tallaght Hospital. When I got to her ward and saw her I thought that she might be dying. The only other person I have spent time with before their death was my grandfather Harry and it felt similar. I wasn't allowed to see my auntie when she was dying from meningitis. I was still a child and repeatedly heard the word 'swelling' as I lingered on the periphery of adult conversations. I really wanted to see her. I can still recall my mental image of this swelling. It was just her perfect face rendered maybe seven or eight times larger than it really was, still smiling. Like a caricature. I also now have an estimation of what her condition might actually have been like, and naturally, the two are worlds apart.

Phil's skin is grey and flaky and looks like it is being irritated by the fluorescent light in the ward. A physiotherapist has come in to take a woman in the neighbouring bed for a walk and he is extremely loud. 'THAT'S RIGHT, OVER TOWARDS EILISH. *ONE LEG* OVER TOWARDS EILISH. UPTALLUPTALLUPTAL-LUPTALL.' Phil was getting increasingly distressed. She couldn't really speak or open her eyes but she would take the necessary minutes to get one or two words out when she was really pushed. I knew what she had been wanting and trying to say for almost ten minutes and then she finally whispered the word 'him' and, having struggled a minute or so more, 'stop'. All she could do apart from that was murmur. But it was constant. Chant like. And the hardest part was that she was trying to communicate the entire time so you were trying to listen the entire time too, listening for a word breaking through that you could take and try to fit into different potential meanings or requests.

She seemed to have the most miniscule increase in energy after she drank some water or juice. Everyone was talking about her swallow and I knew if it stopped working that it would be the beginning of the end. Each time I held the straw to her mouth I could see the apple juice lift a little way out of the glass through it and back down. A tiny bit higher each time but it took so much energy from her. I would watch it so closely and sometimes if she didn't follow the next sip up quick enough her progress would be lost and it would all drop back down into the glass and she'd have to start again. It was a bit like pinball, keeping the ball up with all the levers and barriers, or like the game of trying to keep the balloon off the ground at children's birthday parties, sacrificial bodies strewn over couches and other people, poking it up into the air before touching off the wooden floor. Or like the physio trying to get her neighbour to stand up tall up tall up tall before she slumped back down into her chair.

Phil was in a lot of pain. She was crying and murmuring and sweating and shaking viciously. She could barely open her eyes and when she tried to, often when I asked her to in the middle of a particularly scary memory she seemed to be reliving – just to try and situate her in the room with me – it took about ten active seconds of her trying to open them, to unstick the seal that was smeared across her lids. It was like her body wasn't even helping her any more. Was putting up intentional barriers to her continued existence. Sealing her eyes closed and weakening her throat and sphincter muscles. A real betrayal after eighty-six years of nourishing her and showing her things. Sometimes after drinking some water or juice, the words seemed to come a little easier, though they were still difficult to hear. She cried, begging someone not to force her to eat the mouldy bread and also later begging them not to hit her again.

The woman on the other side of Phil has Alzheimer's, and she asks to go to the bathroom once every five minutes or so. She has hurt her hip and shouldn't really be getting up and down that much. 'Please help me,' she repeats to anyone walking by. And also to any shadow that passes her, I noticed, as her neighbour's curtain was pulled over for a consultation and she mistook the lengthy dark stretch of the blue curtain for a person who could help. For language to lose meaning while muscle loses tone and synapses lose connection has to be the most disorienting experience. The whole system of language on which we've built our interaction and understanding is wiped. And it's not all you. It's me not helping you when you ask. It's me not following up on your requests because they are impossible to do but not to understand or hear. I should've told her that I could hear her. I should've told her that I understood her. Perhaps that would've been enough.

A doctor comes in, shakes our hands firmly and tells Phil and us that it is not a stroke, it is not a brain bleed or a tumour. Or, more accurately, that he seriously doubts it is but will be doing an MRI tomorrow to officially rule that out. He feels confident, he says, that it is something called serotonin syndrome. He is warm, pleasant, direct, honest. He speaks to us and then when he realises Phil is more aware than she initially comes across, he redirects his conversation to her. He is doing everything you would want him to do. He is the kind of doctor that you accidentally latch on to too closely because you are so scared and low. The kind of doctor some patients will gush to and pour out the details of their divorce and difficult upbringing instead of their pain scale like he asked because they haven't received such undivided, caring attention in years. The kind who others, more reserved, would think about later that day warmly and wonder what he is having for dinner.

He says we are lucky, it is good news; it was nearly fatal but we are lucky she was brought in when she was. We are shocked in a way that leans towards euphoria rather than horror because *fatal* is prefaced with *nearly*. He bolsters us to feel good. I believe that he means it. I am still drawn in by the authenticity of his presentation. But he leaves, goes home, and I miss a link. He said we should be happy – I did believe him. I was. So how have I forgotten why?

She has serotonin syndrome. She was not monitored properly upon the upping of her dose of various psych meds. The level of serotonin in her system skyrocketed to the point that she almost died. She is experiencing severe tremors and hallucinations. These will improve, which is what we are told to focus on. Of course we are told to, and why wouldn't we? It seems morbid that I would want to focus on the negative. But I can't help it because Phil is still lying there in agony. She can't communicate, eat, sit up, walk, lift things, or think properly. She has a fever like I have never seen. I can almost feel the heat radiating from her red skin. Everything is jumbled up with her subconscious spilling through in what sound like dark childhood memories that she is reliving. She is scared. She had to immediately come off all meds.

Strip her system. It is a necessary, though extreme measure. And I am angry that nobody has paused with me and said, 'Yes, this is awful'.

*

When Libby Zion, *New York Times* writer Sidney Zion's daughter, who was widely believed to have died from serotonin syndrome, passed away at age eighteen in a New York City emergency room, Sidney Zion described her hospital treatment in animal terms. The intern responsible for her care, resting in an on-call room, ordered the nurses to medically restrain her in her hospital bed in A&E. 'Like a dog,' Sidney Zion wrote. I think of Anna Kavan's writing in her book *Asylum Piece*, of a section that always stays with me, for some reason clings to me. I reread chunks of this book while Phil was recovering from serotonin syndrome because nothing else seemed to describe what I was seeing. She was so hard to reach in those days and weeks that nothing and nobody seemed close to her. Nothing closer than these lines of Kavan's: 'But now I am lying in a lonely bed. I am weak and confused. My muscles do not obey me, my thoughts run erratically as small animals do when they are concerned.'

This weakness and confusion that Phil experienced was shared by others on her ward, dedicated mainly to older women who have experienced strokes. Most of them have to learn to speak and walk again. Each case is unquestionably sad but there is an ease to the linear progression of their recoveries that irks me, no matter how much compassion I try to summon. The language system, lost to these women temporarily, is one they have been acquainted with since they were young children. They are working hard to recover from this aphasia but the system is there waiting for them. It is reliable. In recalling words, stringing sentences together, they are recalibrating their autonomy. It is not easy work but somehow, as I sit and watch them, I have labelled it straightforward work. I have convinced myself that everything is there for them. Resources at their disposal that Phil doesn't have. Some of this might be true. Things we don't even see as resources. Trust, support from social environments, lack of judgement towards their diagnosis. They are taken at face value when they begin to reformulate sentences and I hold that against them.

I feel guilty for doing it but I can't stop myself. I am sitting beside my grandmother and I am so protective of her and I am angry on her behalf and I am letting the weight of that rest, for a moment, in the wrong place. On the wrong people. I don't know where it is supposed to land and I have to take small breaks from carrying it forward, or outward, and in these breaks I think the worst things about good people. Nothing looks out of place when I walk into the ward. Visually, there is no odd one out. Most are lying there. Some are sitting, propped up by a throne of pillows. They all look tired. In terms of charts though, their medical labels, Phil is outside of something. In *Birds' Nest Soup*, which narrates the horror of life in a psychiatric hospital in the Irish midlands in the 1940s and '50s, Hanna Greally writes against this act of labelling. Responding to words like schizophrenia, paranoia and melancholia, she writes, 'The funny thing about those words, they just did not seem to fit those quiet, silent patients who were thus categorised.' Phil is old and tired and her medical diagnoses seem to carry an energy and sense of threat that she does not. My thoughts about these women are similarly offensive. I am labelling their difficulty as ease, their confusion as imminent clarity. I don't want to do that.

Nonetheless, Phil is going a level deeper than most of these women. She is having to wade back into the language of subservience. She is travelling further, where it is darker and colder. Where she is working twice as hard to communicate. Where she is having to bring a dexterity of thought and expression, through sweats and tremors induced by these doctors, to pull together a sentence that says to them, 'No, I am not strong enough to bang an empty 7up bottle off my bedside locker when I need help.' She is working double time to be afforded basic things. Basic courtesy, basic trust, basic material items needed to get through the day, basic authority over her own desires – when she is hungry, when she is thirsty, when she is tired, when she wants to be alone, when she wants to be with a group. Her requests need to be binary.

They need to be loyal to the self in some fundamental way so she doesn't lose all sense of herself while still having a tenuous link to the representative of the oppressive system. She has to convince them that she is deserving of what she wants in a way that doesn't disturb their inchoate view of her but that also doesn't feed into it to the point that they conclude it is unsafe or inappropriate to let her have or do the things she wants.

Phil is wrangling with a trifecta of social stigma – mentally ill, old, and female. It feels as if there is a time capsule of the concept of growth. As if older people aren't growing too. There is a stagnancy to Phil's experience. Her trajectory is not linear but muddled, fractured, jumping back and forth. A gossamer thread linking her to society when living on the periphery of it and then completely shut out when hospitalised.

Similarly for now, our conversation feels like lines fizzling and jumping around a cracked phone screen. Requiring innovative interaction for it to work. Pressing this broken part of the screen, for some unknown reason, brightens up the bottom left corner so you can now tap on the phone icon, and then when you make the call it isn't actually too crackly. A mixture of visual, metaphysical malleability with tangible wiring being physically held. Texting your friend in a different time zone, such quick delivery of messages, but holding, all the while, the cheap broken wire of your charger at an angle so that it will keep you teetering on 3 per cent. The repeated 'bing' of the charge going on and off begins corresponding with the dart of nerve pain shooting up your arm that is tense and spent from holding this tiny wire perfectly still. You lose that perfect angle somehow in the aggression of the stillness, and after a few moments of trying to naturally reclaim the angle, like moving your face slightly to catch the sun, you give up. So you take to ramming the charger into the phone with force and speed, hoping it will just bolt a connection. Just ram it in and it might charge. The pain resonates dull in your elbow when you do this but sometimes it works, so you don't mind. That's what it's like speaking to Phil at the moment. You try to develop habits even though none of your habitual conversation has ever had any patterned response that would justify reusing the approach. You still do. Just because sometimes it works. Sometimes anything works, so you just keep doing everything you can and you know there is no rhyme or reason to the connection, when it is made or when it isn't, so you just keep doing and waiting, randomly connecting, then holding again, strained and hopeful, connecting, waiting again.

The easiest thing about it all is that no matter how tired you get or how futile your repeated change of tactic is, you are numbly content to keep going. It's not in a celebratory way but just a dull, repetitive plugging away for a spark. Worth it for that brief shot of red. Of contact. Warmth. Enough to see you through to the next. Eye contact. Then looking through you. Then finding you again. Then smiling. Then losing you. So much travelling. 'More juice?'

The Springfield Hotel

THE SPRINGFIELD HOTEL WAS A HOTEL IN THE TOWN JUST OVER FROM OURS. But to me, it was four things. The site of four distinct experiences or feelings. The first and earliest, a Sunday carvery there with my family when I was young, maybe twelve or thirteen. I had been given, the day before, some hand-me-downs from the teenage children of my mother's friend. They smelled still of someone else's body and someone else's house and I sat there, in the hotel dining room with my three family members, feeling distinctly out of place. Smelling, as if proof of my alienation, the intimate lives of some other family that I was wearing.

It was the fresh first few months of my period and if the stranger's clothes I wore weren't enough to make me feel out of place at the dinner table, this new clawing ache inside my stomach was. We ate the usual meal. Said the usual things. The foreignness of my clothes and my body was suppressed by the show of normality around me. My sister was being herself, eating each part of her meal separately. My mother was being herself, smiling at any waiter or hotel manager or guest that passed our table, then dropping the smile abruptly when faced with her meal again, her tablemates. My father was being himself, twitching his eyes aggressively to the side every few minutes as if glancing towards the screen of green grass and athletes but really towards the bar below the screen. Everything was normal outside of my body, outside of my outfit. The light though, from the window behind my father's head, softened in that ethereal yellow way that is actually frightening not calming. That is apocalyptic, if your mood allows. The light confirmed, somehow, my feeling of alienation. Commandeered any sadness or discomfort I was withholding in my seat. Poured the sadness over the shoulders of my father, bleached his twitching eye when he next flicked his gaze to the side such that I couldn't really see him. His pupils, even in a shadowed room, when they twitched like this disappeared from sight; like when we roll our eyes, but to the side. But always I would see the veiny white of his empty eyes. Here he rolled his eyes to the side and his pupils seemed to roll all the way out. Out past the glass pane with condensation and into the gravelled car park, for all I knew. Demonic it looked, really. But nobody else stirred. The woman behind him ate apple pie and a young family, tired, collapsed in through the front door and found their way to a table. A cloud passed over, changing the light and his eyes cleared and he was, once again, just a normal man waiting impatiently to be dropped off at the pub on the way home. I would be driven home from there by my mother and my sister would disappear to a friend's house and I would be acquainted, for the first time, with the blistering relief of a hot water bottle, would begin my gentle move towards direct rubber-to-skin contact and welts. The easier choice, numbness as solution.

*

The second engagement with the Springfield Hotel was more abstract. A knowledge of the interior of the building and the details of other lives. When I was a teenager three or four of my friends began working in this hotel, and others like it. So many intimate details of their lives, shared with me at the time, were irrecvocably enmeshed with my visual memory of the interior design of the Springfield Hotel. I didn't feel responsible for my friends in the way I felt responsible for my mother but could feel, nonetheless, the weight of their own family issues. Thinking of one friend in particular I could picture, only, this young man, pouring pints behind the bright wood-panelled bar for lairy older men, the wood tinging green in some lights. Could feel, only, a conspiracy on their part, or complicity. Couldn't help but blame them a little for whatever conversations about women and their disposability that were spilling over into his young ears. Could picture, only, this young man folding heavy-duty white table linen and pulling back heavy velvet curtains for sash windows and placing heavy, for their purpose at least, napkins on the dining tables in certain shapes. Could think only of the textiled contradiction of these threads of luxury or weight and his thin, cheap boxers in bright colours, or the thin line of yellow around the long-term underarm sweat patch on his work shirt that, yes, had been washed, but still, that stain of old sweat. Or the almost see-through rib of his white ankle socks that I saw him wearing one day, with his uniform, peeking out from behind his shiny, pointy black shoes.

*

Third, the second wedding of my first boyfriend's father. A wedding that my mother bought me a dress for and some small heels and curled my hair for and drove me to. I was on the pill now, in less pain. I was wearing my own clothes. I was feeling distinctly myself until she dropped me to the door of the hotel and, like a bolt back to my childhood sleepovers when I would lie awake in other people's houses and wonder what she was doing, I asked, leaning back into the car to grab my bag, urgently really, 'What are you going to do for the afternoon?' No answer would've satisfied me probably. I would've sought out loneliness or cause for concern in any plan she may have half formed. I don't even remember her answer. I just remember sitting in the fold of extended family members that welcomed me as their own. Worrying about my mother. Feeling guilty. And then later that evening, watching my boyfriend's mother, his father's first wife, sitting at a table speaking to the mother of the bride – laughing and smiling. I felt anger. Why wasn't my mother brave enough to leave? She should've left by now. We shouldn't still be doing this. Enduring this. Even though she will pick me up later this evening she shouldn't be bringing me back there.

*

The final memory, which eclipses without effort the other three, is of Phil being sectioned at this hotel. She refused to engage with the doctors, would not open her door to them or answer their calls. The police also. In response, the police contacted the local taxi service, knowing she often ordered a taxi to Tesco to drive her home with her shopping. The police told the taxi service to alert them when Phil next phoned. She phoned for a taxi to the Springfield Hotel one Sunday lunchtime so she could enjoy a carvery there. The entire thing is infuriating, the interaction between the doctors and police. But what upsets me most is that the taxi driver took her all the way there first. The fact that she paid him. The fact that she queued up in the line for the carvery, tray in hand. The fact that she was halfway through a meal, hadn't even finished her dinner, when the Gardaí walked into the hotel and removed her. My anger is lit up picturing the gaudy, beaming high-vis of their uniform, the cold discarded food on her plate. Tender chicken breast half pulled from itself with a fork and left. The scene abandoned.

They made a decision to humiliate her. When they arrived at her table she spoke first, soft under her breath and said, 'I will walk out myself. I will meet you outside.'

Hell Is Other People

SPACES OF ORIGIN AND DESTINY ARE SPOKEN ABOUT BY PEOPLE WHO INFLUENCE ME. People I listen to by default, who talk about cosmological and evolutionary leaps. Some talk about imaginative paradigms shifting. They talk about them from the safe house of university offices, the sound, somehow, structure of a sky-high library. I listen from these places too. I speak back in these places. Slowly at first, unsure. Then with confidence, a little. Others, people I love, inhabit the leap, dance in the space of it. People with

133

tenure-track positions tell me that the centrality of new imaginative narratives are exemplified in things like Elizabeth DeLoughrey's account of water's mutability. Others feel on a visceral level the mutability of water. They feel the shift and shrivel of their lithium-laced bodies that aren't absorbing enough water. It is the difference between practice and theory. Babies mimic their care givers and it seems, all in all, the best way to learn. Listening to Phil has been the best way to learn these things.

If I discount the undercurrent of divinity in her narrative, Phil has also taught me something about bodily autonomy, or having a body, when she repeatedly told me bodies are not durable, bodies are not durable. She has prompted me, in her consistent disdain for the physical form, to realise that my body is not all I think it is. It feels like a pulsing, celestial version of my mother telling me as a child that nobody was watching me anyway when I tried to dance awkwardly at a family function, or when she made me try on a dress over my school uniform in a shop instead of queuing for the changing rooms like everyone else. It is as authoritative and final as my mother's response in the clothing shop when I would present her with a top that I liked. I would tell her I liked it. 'Do you?' she would say back, my first introduction to rhetorical questioning and fashion-related judgement.

I am confronted with Phil's indifference to her body, ashamed almost that so many of my obstacles to joy are centred around mine.

When I hear the pad of my bare feet on the wooden floorboards as I walk to the bathroom in the morning, I am disgusted. When I can taste my own saliva, though my breath is fresh, I am disgusted. When markers of my own existence show themselves to me in these unavoidable physical ways, the default response is to be repulsed.

These are the descriptions I share with my therapist when she asks me to expand on the idea of not feeling great about myself. I don't know what she was expecting but I smile nervously at her on my laptop screen when I finish talking. There are other things I want her to know but I don't want to say them. I am happy to share them with her but it is dangerous to let them take centre stage in my mind. When I let these ideas take words and leave my mouth they cling back onto me in ways that reveal themselves when she is gone and the Zoom meeting has ended. I keep smiling at her. I tell her I don't know what intrusive thoughts are. Don't know whether the feelings I have been having recently would neces-sarily count as intrusive thoughts.

She asks me how I feel. The Zoom glitches mean I often look sad to her when I am not and she asks quite directly, 'What about that makes you sad?', confident in the visual cues of digital body language. I reserve my rejection of this claim of sadness for certain moments because it seems like a cop out that I would say I am not sad to my therapist on a regular basis. Surely it would seem like I am lying. I don't even know if I'm sad anyway, unless I am crying. I just tell her what stands out most from the intrusive thought. The amount of blood. My therapist wonders how often I have these intrusive thoughts and I let her know it has been quite regular in the past year or so. She tells me to picture my intrusive thoughts as clouds floating across the sky. She tells me to imagine I am lying on the grass and looking up at the sky. And there are clouds. They are moving slowly and steadily across the sky. They are my intrusive thoughts. And I can see them and I can recognise them but they are just passing by. And I am watching. This seems helpful, immeasurably helpful, I promise her – affecting a tone of almost looking forward to my next intrusive thought so I could flex this new cumulus muscle.

The day arrived. I was standing at the kitchen sink and the knife jammed in the drawer in a way that I immediately pictured the drawer to be something else. No warning. I bypassed my imagination and looked to the real sky. It was all cloud. No blue and no shade of grey either so I could decipher a dark-grey thunder cloud passing ominously by something lighter, less threatening. Not even that. Not even shades of clouding. Not even shades of intrusion. Just blanket grey. People confined and incarcerated talk about the sky all the time. In *Asylum Piece*, Anna Kavan describes things 'vanishing into the upper blue', talks about the sky as 'hard as a blue plate'. The impact of that is something I know. What should be free and endless and open is ceramic and hard and smacks against me. If I were to adopt Phil's line of thinking on the uselessness of the body, I might find a shortcut to recovery. Although, I think to myself, perhaps she thought the same.

*

Words my grandmother had her nurses print out the dictionary definition of:

Atrocious
Reprehensible
Seize
Culminate
Concede
Paradox (medical, cultural and computational definitions)
Adamant
Demand
Vitiate
Fait accompli
Pedant

I could find another lesson in these words, their definitions, their companion words when I search them in my thesaurus, the fact that her nurses were printing them for her. I would make a whole world of learning out of that. Draw them out on a page like a family tree of verbal incarceration. They might look like lungs. They might breathe around the next sentence, which is hers and beats still like a steady heart. *You attempt to deny your complicity in the fallen state by projecting it outside yourself.*

*

I was never an avid reader as a child in the way you hear some people describe: disappearing into books, letting those worlds swallow them whole for an entire afternoon. I have to admit to myself that I often prefer spending time with the things people have written on paper than the people themselves and this is probably as close as I will get to that voracious reading appetite.

Rónán's mother, Pauline, died at the end of March, and when I was in her bedroom choosing an outfit for her to wear in her coffin, I found notes she had written to me. I took photographs of them on my phone and my camera. And then I spent twenty minutes trying to figure out whether to pack a bra for the undertaker to dress her dead body in. I was crying as I was searching for a bra with no underwire, so the moment wasn't void of emotion, but it was practical nonetheless and lacking. My care was still there in that I was inherently wedded to an idea of comfort. I was choosing soft socks and a bra with no underwire and a vest for under her top. But it was just an idea of warmth I was fabricating. It was as useless as people putting images of a fireplace on their laptop or television screen as they attempt to recreate ritual or Christmas cheer. The hearth draws you in because it is elemental not pixelated. It is a loser's game to chase it. I knew in the back of my mind I was choosing clothes for her body to be burned in.

Fait accompli.

Phil was already dead when my mam called to tell me.

Pauline was already dead by the time we were speeding down the motorway at 3 a.m. to try and catch her before she went.

Last year, when my mother called to tell me Phil was getting sicker, it prompted Rónán to some kind of action. This is why I could hear him lighting the fire so early in the day as my mother ended the call. Early white afternoon light pouring in on the red of the premature flame. The intention is always comfort-based when the fire is lit early in the day, but the outcome is often uneasy. Something small that we know in a place or time where we don't know it. Some slight, uncanny domestic discrepancy. We always forget that it is upsetting, in the end, to light the fire early. Always do it again when something bad happens. So it has come, instead of a source of comfort, to embody a ritual of domestic disturbance. Preparing for something too soon.

Nostalgia is only a mechanism of protection and it is only needed in acute moments like these. The rest of the time we are simply gorging on it. I could've read meaning into anything I liked in Pauline's bedroom. The Sharpie she used to write my name and phone number was fading by the time she reached the 'y' in Molly. That doesn't matter, but I remember it. She had written on the side of her wardrobe that Rónán was allergic to penicillin. In her kitchen, I moved a pan from the draining board and found an unopened packet of Spider-Man napkins underneath. These physical discoveries shock, charged with energy. They are all speaking all the time, these objects. Telling me what they missed, what they were meant for. In that house it is easy to feel like a character in a bad book. It is easy to feel at the mercy of a careless writer. Painful objects are strewn around and charged with insurmountable power. You would never do that to your characters.

*

I am gorging on nostalgia as I read through these notes of Phil's too. The next lesson will be to teach myself to stop. I think I am already in the process of learning this because I am less fixated on the deep philosophical enquiries she has scrawled on the back of hospital leaflets and more buoyed by the small squares of white paper that each have short cohesive sentences.

Plant like: give them what they need and they grow. (*Plant* and *like* are underlined.)

What kind of music does your Dad like? Whatever sucks

Exact, an exact description: precise, accurate, correct, faithful, close, true, literal, strict, perfect, careful, meticilous, conscientious, scrupulus. (*perfect* is underlined.)

Most of the notes are interspersed with the reminder that *hell is other people* and it is starting, in itself, to feel like a suitable reminder whenever it appears. There is almost a rhythm to its recurrence.

*

In college, everyone keeps telling me about ruptures in chronological time. It keeps coming up. When we talk about trauma, when we talk about climate narratives. It feels like a life jacket for the first year of hearing about it. Then, slowly, the fact that we are still speaking about it, still only speaking about it seems to somehow dilute it. Or organise it, perhaps. Putting one word after another on a page, in person, in colloquium meetings with mini croissants and fruit and drip coffee on demand, that say in a linear, ordered, translatable

fashion important-work-ruptures-chronological-
narratives-blurs-boundaries-between-memory-
self-and-other seems suddenly to be something
we are flying in the face of with academia. Are
we lining these facts up? Straightening, ordering
and proofreading them in our publications? Are
we sharpening the blur we pretend to revere by
staring so intently at it? Where else can we look?
What embodies this blur? What else can we question, look at, listen to, that explains the rupture?
That is inherently achronological? Such that we
understand the blur a little better? Slip into it,
slide, jelly-like and unmoored. No root, no end,
no floor. Circles only. Slides.

Trauma isn't linear. Life isn't linear. I have
already been told this. Phil told me. She used to
send me text messages that mapped and charted
her thought processes, partially at least.

*'That Sad Tomorrow Will Never Come To
You! ... he Made a Catastrophic Mistake! He did
not recognise "Me" and Lied To "My" Face! ...
Nobody Lies To God and Lives To Tell The Tale!'*

She matched in songs afterwards, that she
liked me to listen to while I read her messages.

The song here was Dusty Springfield, 'The Look of Love'. *The look that time can't erase*, I heard as I read her note. Her note that said she was not recognised. More important than being the note that says she is God, it is the note that says she was not recognised. Her doctors were focused on the God delusion. I was focused on the misrecognition. Each in their way timeless, cyclical.

For her written definition of pedant she included three entries:

> *A person who insists on a strict adherence to formal rules or literal meaning at the expense of the wider view.*
>
> *A person who rates academic learning or technical knowledge above everything.*
>
> *A person who is obsessed by a theory, a doctrinaire.*

Alongside other teachers I've had Phil would probably qualify as a doctrinaire, but then again, hell is other people.

The limits to learning in an educational institution are far more stifling than a psychiatric hospital. I have learned much more from Phil and the different people she has lived with. And it is the same lesson both institutions are trying to teach. Identify and then break a mould and then piece it back together anew. The inhabitants of one institution, professors, require that you break the mould in specific ways, break it into a distinct number of pieces, make the cut at certain right angles. Do it this way. The inhabitants of the other institution say, smash it on the ground, bend down to your hunkers and see what it looks like there on the floor in the multiple, unique shards it has made of itself.

Hell is other people seems a given. Which ones we listen to and learn from does not have to be prescribed. For the most part, people who are being silenced and sedated will have something to teach you if you can be fluid about what it is to learn and make your peace with the fact that even these people, even your greatest teachers, especially your greatest teachers, are hell.

Death, a Sky
Behind Her

EVERYTHING WAS ENGINES. The runway looked glamorous in the way it does, can, at dusk. The runway lights bled up when the plane turned slowly into the glint of the Boston skyscrapers.

A big engagement ring of a plane dropping through layers of cloud, stepping down out of glint and twinkle into engine and smoke. A debutante arriving down a staircase and promptly disappointing.

Outside the window, a yacht passed across the Boston harbour at unexpected speed, moving to the right as the plane taxied down the runway. Everything engine. Everything in the city engine, and the violet sky tucking it all in. Sickly and churning and sweet, still. Everything could put you to sleep. Everything was gaseous, Parma-Violet noxious. Sweet still. Heavy and sweet, if a little dangerous.

My neighbour ate twenty-four miniature carrots from a small plastic bag during the taxi and then let her head drop back to the chair on take-off. Neck slick to the headrest's curve. My head stayed up like a small baby. A small, capable baby.

Above the city of engines, a bed of white cloud. Resting on the bed, an indigo-blue sky absorbing a grey orb of light from a full, plump Aries moon. And Phil somewhere out there.

There was a baby at the gate before boarding with a flutter of bright-red hair on her small head. She looked almost too small to hold her own head up. Yet she was standing. Holding on to the chair and moving herself between it and her mother's leg.

Once I was in my plane seat, looking back at the panel of windows that held our waiting bay, it seemed like a cinema palette charting the colours of her prospective life. She was on the plane with me somewhere, sleeping maybe or enquiring about apple juice or corn snacks. But the shades of honey, marigold, blush barley and pale peach of that waiting area, panelled by windows and held in the same violet sky as the flickering city lights, all hunkered below the higher indigo, suggested in their blended brightness something to come.

The energy I use to hold my neck up against the push of gravitational force during take-off might be the small bit of life force Phil has left in me, now activated in her absence. Or activated in this small child, perhaps. It isn't always so straightforward, if it does happen. I would be more inclined to believe that life as it drains away is siphoned off elsewhere. It might happen on some coordinates that your descendant passes. That crossing might be the strike of lightning. That at most. The red-headed baby might be Phil. I might be witnessing that. Not taking anything with me, wherever I go. Or taking anything on. No. That would weigh me down. I would rather float up a little if I could, touch the grey orb of light, feel all by myself this time the glow of the plump moon.

I had never seen a moon set before.

The moon stayed with me for the entire journey until we were a little way out from the end, when it sank slowly below the cloud bed. The celestial realm.

*

Maybe there are new colours now. Light pinks and pastels. Or new names for colours. Wherever she went I am not concerned with that. With knowing where it is or who else is there. I don't think that way. Find no comfort in it. If it was a certain colour, though, I would find peace in that. If the whole process of life and death was one colour bleeding into another. If the entire background of wherever she is now is washed *as she arrives* with a new shade. If it was a cloudy-blue late-evening sky that changes, when you look at it against the cool white of island walls, to a hazy purple. If she were the cool island rock. If death, a sky behind her, was one broad stroke of a paintbrush, one swash of light, pastel colour. Wet still from the paintbrush, from the rain. The paper, soft, could rip. But won't because we won't hold it, we'll just look at it. Watch the purple settle, stiffen. I would like that. If she was set, then, on the lilac scene like a beautiful collage. I would like that.

Depending on Phil's outfit, the collage might change. Her blue shirt and light-pink trousers *would* have a purple background. It would be blue-pink-purple like baby memories – like baby dolls and baby cartoons and baby crewneck jumpers in the '90s. If it was the photo of her in her cream and light-brown midi dress with cut-out sides standing in front of the Eiffel Tower, it would be a lime-green background, or maybe fluorescent yellow. It would be a lemon-lime shock. It would have to be. If it was any of the black-and-white photographs of her and my grandfather Harry in any number of heavy, quality, long overcoats, hand in hand, or at least side by side, crossing O'Connell Bridge, captured by the man on the bridge, it would be a deep red. A deep blush of big love. If it was the photo of her with her mousy-blonde long hair and cream cardigan painting a canvas that I, the viewer of the photograph, cannot see, but with her own children peering over her shoulder, privy to the sight, the art lesson – it would be everything multicoloured, wish-washed, zigzagged. It would be colour flourished, overlapped, melted.

In Phil's last months I was living and studying in Massachusetts. A couple of weeks before she died my housemates taught me how to collage. We used old *New Yorker* magazines, which felt equally indulgent and destructive. I struggled with the process, leaving too much white on my page. To my mind it left room for imagination but it was gently explained to me that texture is the desired approach with collage, not gaps. I was taking a biography writing class at the same time and one of my classmates was writing her biography on Otto Ege and biblioclasm, the act of destroying books. I never made the connection. On another day of errands I was in the art supplies shop, Michaels, with my supervisor's youngest daughter, Afrah. She bought glitter slime and a 'wreck everything' journal, another purposeful act of biblioclasm. Driving home, the sky could've been ripped like a page too. Like there was something else behind it. A white page. The edge of a cloud crept into the very corner of my passenger seat window as we sat at a traffic light and it felt like a corner of a page that the paint missed.

*

The weeks that I spent in Amherst before Phil's death were made a little softer in that my supervisors, Malcolm and Katherine, are married and extended real kindness to me as a family. Katherine drove me to the post office the day before I flew home for Phil's funeral in April. I was posting a book to my sister, Kerrie, in Canada. Phil's death had pushed forth an in utero urgency. Kerrie was still pregnant but now I was flying home and wouldn't see her until August, at which point the book *The First Forty Days*, which details foods that are nourishing for the mother after birth, would categorically expire. By that time, feet now in her womb would already have outgrown certain Babygros.

In the car with my supervisor, we dropped Afrah off to Irish dancing first. I remember Irish dancing being so vividly rigid. Arms flat to my side, in gentle fists. Legs going wild. Afrah is getting taller all the time.

I was back in Ireland between semesters and they visited us last summer. Rónán and I brought both their girls, Anoushka and Afrah, down to the field to collect some salad. Rónán lunged down a steep incline and Afrah followed, with abandon, and tumbled forward onto the grass. Her legs crumpled in a way that saved her and she bounced back up quickly, like she was dancing. She looked back at me with her large baseball cap and small orange crop top and said, 'Sometimes I do silly things like that,' and I felt the immense pleasure of knowing someone as they grow into themselves. The next time she visits she will probably be able to make the jump, or if she can't, she probably won't turn back to me and narrate her inner monologue about her own falling, her own rising, her own silliness, her own developing character.

After we dropped Afrah to her class, I stayed with Katherine as she ran some errands. We picked Afrah up again and then waited outside Whole Foods for about thirty minutes for the convenient click-and-collect option to collect the fish for their dinner. Katherine apologised a few times as if I had anything more to do that evening than pack my bag, wait for the morning and get my bus to the airport. Fly home. Bury Phil. The apology was kind but it was empty. Empty because she remembered something I had said weeks before to her. That when I am depressed or having a hard time I like nothing better than being the passenger in the car of a woman I know and trust, in the sunshine preferably, the particular warmth of a car, as they get things done. The original warm, safe car being my mother's. She told me a few days later, as we messaged after Phil's funeral, that she had half-driven me around Amherst on that warm evening on purpose because she remembered this. I told my mother a few weeks later on the phone and it was like a gift. Like one mother nodding to another.

Phil's ashes are in my bedroom in a green container that I described to my friend Layla, when she asked, as similar in colour and material to a watering can but different, of course, in every other way. The roses from Phil's funeral are tucked in beside the box of her ashes because the woman working at the crematorium asked me, after the service, if I'd like to keep them and dry them and I said yes. Partially because I wanted to but also because I wanted to be told what to do and how to do it that day. She talked me through the process of drying roses. It is probably the clearest window of memory from the entire week.

*

When we arrived home after the funeral, a neighbour gave us crab claws. It was the first time I had eaten them, which is probably why the memory sticks. Rónán served me a plate with crab claws in garlic butter, asparagus and fresh salad. I had a glass of white wine too. It felt new in and of itself. New and nice to be eating something different. Nice is all it was for a bit until, just over half-way through the meal, it reminded me of Phil. It reminded me so suddenly and viscerally of her that tears started dripping down my face. I cried slow then fast. Fast and relentless. Nothing to do with me, these tears. Sudden and rushing. Something opened up with the crab claws that the man in the boat, who I always watch from our kitchen window, collects. Everything cracked in a way that every song was her. 'Nights on Broadway' by Candi Staton was playing. Everything worth noticing was her. Like the evening was being shrouded in her.

All that washed over me was the knowledge that she would love to be there. She would love to be eating that food. She would be singing that song. Would be dancing. Her and Rónán would be dancing. I would be watching. I would be smiling. How had I not thought of this before? Of her enjoying the life I've made? Enjoying the normal moments I enjoyed. Not the visits that catered to her. The idea of a visit that never happened. But the Friday evenings we shared, Rónán and I, at home. I had never thought of her in these. Not of her being in these. I had enjoyed these times and thought, during them, of a different her in a different place. A different her and me in a different place together.

I patted my recent memory for an image of her in my world, like someone patting their pockets looking for their wallet or phone. I could see her in my mother's apartment on Christmas Day a few years ago. We wore matching pyjamas, like the rest of the country, like we had all signed some invisible contract not to be ashamed of ourselves any more, although we should've been. I could find her sitting in a wheelchair in a shopping centre eating an ice cream. On the corner of Stephen's Green looking at my uncle's artwork on the railings. She was nowhere in my world.

The closest she had come to me before she died was a scheduled call that one of her nurses was going to arrange in the early stages of the first lockdown. I phoned at exactly 7 p.m. as they had asked me to. I knew there would be a slim chance it would be a video call. Everything was as it came. Maybe video, maybe not. Maybe a long chat, maybe a sentence. Maybe I could bring my phone into the sitting room and Rónán could say hi to her. Maybe that wouldn't suit. I was ready for any version of events and ready to be grateful for them too. The call lasted sixteen seconds. I returned to the sitting room after to find Rónán in his best white shirt, waiting. Dressing for the occasion, for the matriarch, as I often did, was starting to rub off on him. Later that evening, as I stood in the kitchen with a head torch on, trying to work the turmeric stain out of his shirt, nothing about it felt wrong. It is the closest she got to visiting us. We were dressed and ready for her digital arrival.

*

For me the marker of a new year is looking out my bathroom window in early April. To the left, seeing my neighbour Ciaran's chip van in his yard with the hatch window open for the first time. The van is being cleaned out, made ready to move down to the seafront for the summer. Tourist boats populate the seascape right in front of me so that I can no longer tell the time of day, as I could in the grey, cold winter months, by the steady coming and going of the good, year-round boat. The eight o'clock departure, midday arrival, four o'clock departure, seven o'clock arrival. The days are longer and bluer, brighter, and the boats keep endlessly coming and going. Everything is one long day in the summer (and if you aren't ready for it, it feels like it will destroy you). One real day feels like three full days; feels chopped twice: once at mid-morning, once mid-afternoon. Living is tripled in April. Every time I lie in the bath I am looking at a perfect blue square in the same Velux window. I can only see sky when I am submerged. I am certain that this is happiness and that I have found something uniquely helpful in this shape and colour.

Hours after my bath I stand in the bathroom and look out the window again. The small yellow rectangle of buttery light is still sitting inside the sky-blue chip van. It is framed, the van, by the darkening sky and sea, so it seems, when I glance past it, like the yellow rectangle is hovering on the horizon. Yesterday. Last year's cleaning out of the chip van feels as close as yesterday. As far as the horizon. The desk I work at in the morning gets the sunrise. It is a large, white, empty desk that I keep clean. The dried roses from Phil's funeral are the only thing on the desk. Months ago, Rónán asked me not to move them. He liked the way they lay there, the way the light lay there on top of them. He wanted me to remind him to take a photograph but I purposefully have not. I am not moving them when I clean either and instead watch the dust build up around them. It is a clean, neat shrine. The sunlight shows up every particle of dust. I have touched the roses in the evening, curtains closed, and they are cold. I have touched them gently when I write in the morning and they are warm in the sun. It is almost like a resuscitation.

It is Phil's one-year anniversary today. The thirteenth of April. I wonder if she has anything left to teach me now, so far away for so long. I find less and less meaning as I read through her notes and ideas, likely because of the sheer volume of them. The first few pages are revelatory but the revelations keep coming. It is as though I am a young teenager with the lawnmower cutting the grass and I am unable to control the lead. I am taken at first by the smell of the freshly cut grass but then, quickly enough, I cannot wind it around my arm or the lawnmower handle as easily as adults do. I cannot lasso it across the lawn in front of me with strength or success.

Two gardens come to mind. The back garden of my childhood home where I learned what cut grass smelled like and how to cut it. And Phil's back garden. I don't remember the back garden in Phil's old home in Blackrock. I remember only the steep curve of her front-garden wall; how we climbed it as children and seemed for a moment to defy gravity. The boxy car in the driveway. I remember walking into her sitting room, but only as if someone were holding a blank page in my direct line of sight. All I can see is on the periphery and it is soft couch edges, tassels on the corners of large rugs, the curved edges of tables and the outline of the fireplace. There are creams, light pinks and muddy greens in my memory. It is the garden of her most recent home that I do know. What I remember of it is almost the perfect inverse of my memory of her old home. I can look right at it, head on, but the edges now are already unclear.

When I got my first camera phone I took a photo of Phil's back garden. She was in the hospital and we were checking on her house. It was filled with stacks of food, multiples of every utensil: four salad spinners, nine graters, twelve colanders. All stacked on a warm mahogany dresser whose beauty I only see now as it sits in my cousin's house as a statement piece in an otherwise muted room, vinyl stacked on the top shelves and the small chubby hands of her young child playing with its lower drawer handles while he tells us a story or sings us a song, holding on to his great-grandmother's furniture. I wonder what furniture Cissie had.

My photo of Phil's garden is taken from her kitchen window as I stand by the sink. We forgot to lift the blind every other time we checked the house. The times we emptied the fridge, moved the post from the hallway, put different lamps on. I opened the blind to look at the garden. The bodies of small dead flies from last summer were gathered in the corner of the windowsill, maybe three or four of them. The main stretch of the windowsill had been cleaned, on a previous visit, but the arm had never extended the cloth all the way into the corner, populated by these minor deaths.

It was shaded slightly by the blind's edge but that wasn't the reason it hadn't been cleaned. It had been seen, looked on with dead certainty and clarity but something in the act of being viewed made the corner so remote as to be almost unreal.

The grass wasn't grass like I knew it. It was hip-height now and hay-like. The full garden was thick with it so I couldn't tell how green it was at the root, ground level. What I looked at was blond, soft and light, blowing in the breeze. Phil had left a white plastic clothes horse in the garden and the blond grass had grown up through its rails and above them. At the back wall, a bright pink rose bush was bursting up and out. It covered the length of the wall and grew up above it, setting a new horizon.

In my early teenage notebooks about missing Phil or trying to understand her there is a note from this day. Its subheading tells me I was looking at her garden for the first time in a long time and the entry says, 'Grass long enough to meet my hair. I would plait them together and stay forever.' It is strange to read that. To see that my teenage self, standing in Phil's house, missed her then as much as I do now, almost thirty and sitting at my desk on the one-year anniversary of her death. I have been growing my hair out from a buzz cut this winter and spring. I have felt it creeping around my ears, which I found irritating until now. The desire remains, unchanged, to grow and brush my hair, and plait it into that long grass. To feel grounded and rooted that way. Facing the wall of loud flowers, shouting over each other, front row, no running away, no need to.

My grandmother said that mistakes are corrected before they are made. And that only we correct our own. I suppose she is saying 'nothing is wrong'. I suppose she is saying 'everything is and will be okay'. I suppose she is saying it doesn't matter who lives in her house now or what length the grass is, just that I am growing my hair and knowing what it could mean.

Acknowledgements

I'D LIKE TO THANK MY AGENT MARIANNE GUNN O'CONNOR. Her guidance, support and encouragement has made this book what it is. She has carved out space for this book from our very first conversation and helped to cultivate its strange and natural development. Thanks to Ian Maleney for early rigorous edits and friendship.

Thanks to Arnold Thomas Fanning for welcoming my voice into a very specific conversation. To Declan, Danny and everyone at The Stinging Fly for telling me I was a writer before I felt like one and publishing my first essay. Thanks to Eimear, Laura and Jess at Banshee and Dean and Emily at The Pig's Back for publishing two others.

Thanks to Layla for always listening. Thanks to Tricia and Brian for, in the most tangible way, making this book possible. Thanks to Katherine, Malcolm and Peggy for all of their support. Thanks to Deirdre, Djinn, Leonie and everyone who has worked on this book with such care. Thanks to Pablo and Denise.

There were difficult moments in working on this book when I was reading concurrent histories; state and family. Noticing overlapping dates of certain atrocities in hospital environments and the location of family members would've been more painful again had I not been making the discovery in the pages of well-written books by people like Catherine Cox, Damien Brennan and others. While the material they work with is difficult the goodness of their intention courses through their writing and both taught and comforted me massively as I wrote this book.

For encouragement at different turns thanks to Doireann Ní Ghríofa, Sara Baume, Niamh Campbell, Louise Nealon, Nicole Flattery, Colin Barrett, Chris Morash, Colin Graham, Hilary Woods, Liam Harrison & all at Tolka.

Thanks to my mam for being the ultimate (and coolest) cheerleader.

Thanks to my sister for being my first big love!

Thanks to my baby niece Ruba for embodying in one giggle some kind of destination that this book is trying to reach.

Thanks to Phil for putting no strict shape on what a grandmother-granddaughter relationship need look like and pouring so much into my world in the process.

Lastly, thanks to Rónán, who amongst so many other wonderful things, always believes whole-heartedly in new versions of me before they have arrived.